My Hero Wears A Robe

My Hero Wears A Robe

Karen Cannon

IngramSpark

CONTENTS

1 | CHAPTER 1   1

2 | Life Happens   3

3 | Fast Forward   5

4 | The Engagement   6

5 | The Honeymoon   10

6 | The Saga Begins   14

7 | Getting Married   22

8 | One Day A Week   27

9 | The Men and Women That
Nourish Our Spiritual Health   30

10 | Learning to be a Minister's Wife   34

CONTENTS

11 | THE PEDESTAL 40

12 | DON'T ASK / DON'T TELL 42

13 | PARSONAGE PATTER 45

14 | A WORLD OF CHANGES 53

15 | GRRRRRRR...THE MOVE 56

16 | TRANSITIONING 74

17 | WEDDINGS 79

18 | A DIVORCED CHRISTIAN. HOW
COULD THAT BE?! 87

19 | An Unwanted Bride 89

20 | THE HILLBILLY WEDDING 92

21 | JULY 4TH WEDDING 96

22 | HARLEY DUDE 99

23 | THE WEDDING THAT WASN'T 101

24 | FUNERAL FOLLY 106

25 ❚ YOU'RE BURYING HIM WHERE? 109

26 ❚ EVIL? 111

27 ❚ A GHASTLY graveside 113

28 ❚ RANDOLPH 115

29 ❚ WALT REDMOND, JR. 119

30 ❚ OUTLANDISH COMPLAINTS 132

31 ❚ Oh God, Please No More Meetings 138

32 ❚ A Letter to the Bishop (It is all about me!) 141

33 ❚ The Next Chapter 144

34 ❚ Questions for Jeff 146

CHAPTER 1

I wanted to call this first section the "Foreword", but then you might not have read it. I used to flip past the "foreword pages" of a book. Then one day I accidentally read one and to my surprise I found that it was an integral part of understanding the entirety of the book. Now I am aware of the importance of having a bit of background information. It allows the reader to better understand a little of what and who the book is about. So, before we jump into the craziness of the lives involved herein, I will enlighten you with the pertinent information. I hope this will enable you to "walk in my shoes" and understand my perspective. Now, enjoy chapter 1, even though it really is the "foreword". Do not skip it just because I revealed its true identity.

It was the summer of 1979. We met in the Narthex of the church I had been attending since the age of two. I was eighteen years old. He was 23 years old, handsome, full of insight, energy and love for God. He had come to "my" church, where he would serve for several years as an assistant to our minister.

When we met, he had not yet graduated from Seminary. He was just a regular guy sharing his love for God with anyone he could get to listen. I got to know him, not because of what he did, but because of who he was. He was my friend. His full-time job, at the time was as the Regional Director of "Youth For Christ", a Christian organization that met with students in the local public High Schools. The day we met, he invited me to become a volunteer to help with the Campus Life club in the high school that I had just graduated from. I had been a member of this club a year or so prior to my graduation and knew it was a great organization. Still, I do not know why I said yes. I was very shy. The only answer I can come up with is that God was preparing me for what was to come, many years later.

Life Happens

As anyone over forty knows, time flies when you are having children and trying to stay ahead of the bills. Juggling family and work can be both rewarding and difficult. Paying bills on a limited budget is the bane of most people's lives. We all know that just when you think you've "got it all together", there will be some unexpected expense, like soccer, karate and bowling. Caps and gowns, class rings, teenaged drivers on the insurance and the list goes on and on and on! It felt like the important things in my life were slipping away and there was nothing I could do about it. Half of my life was over. Now, THAT was a sobering thought. The face I was looking at in the mirror was not the young, pretty, sexy, thirty something mom that I was used to seeing. (Okay, NOT the pretty and sexy part, just the thirty something part). No, the face I was seeing was looking more and more like MY mom! At the very least, it is safe to say I was a little stressed!

This is where the antidepressants come in. I know what you are thinking and Yes, I AM a Christian. Yes, I KNOW God has this! Yes, I am praying about my sanity! I also know that God made many gifted and intelligent people, who have become doctors and scientists, that have figured out how to help people. I am also smart enough to know when I need help.

I was happy. Really, I was. My hormones were just having a difficult time.

3

Fast Forward

Twenty-five years later, due to martial difficulties that spiraled out of control in our lives, we found ourselves separated from our spouses and heading for divorce courts. Our friendship began to grow. We commiserated and found comfort in our mutual losses as well as the pain and sadness of divorce. We spent many afternoons and evenings talking about what went wrong in our marriages. We began hanging out together sharing tears and words of support. We discussed our friendship, our past successes, mistakes, and our aspirations for the future. As the days turned into months, a more personal relationship developed between us and, as best friends, we found ourselves falling in love.

When one door closes, another opens, and it seems that God had a plan for us.

4

The Engagement

Jeff and I had been dating for eleven months and it was quickly approaching a New Year. We had been invited by some friends of ours to join them for dinner and a party at one of the local hotels for a New Year's Eve event. I had always spent New Year's Eve just trying to stay awake long enough to see the New York City Times Square New Year's Eve Ball drop at the stroke of midnight. Going to an actual New Year's Eve party was an exciting notion to me. So, I put on my sexiest little black dress (which all women should have in their closet) and prepared for my date. The dress was tea length with a wispy hemline. The top of it had spaghetti straps and a "v" neckline that was lined with a single strand of beads and sequins. I felt like a princess waiting for her knight in shinning armor to come and whisk her away. I know how lame that is, but seriously, it is every girls dream no matter how old she is.

As excited as I was, I was a little tense about the evening, worrying that I would not be able to stay awake until midnight. I was determined that I would not be a "party pooper".

Besides, who could fall asleep with all the partying and noise? When we arrived, we checked in with the reservation desk and were shown to our table. I noticed that Jeff was a little anxious but figured it was my dazzling personality (and dress) that had him on edge. We shared a lovely dinner but still had two more hours to go before midnight.

Due to the creeping of the hour and the glasses of wine that I had consumed, I was beginning to feel the heaviness of my eyelids. The sleepy bug was rearing its ugly head. I knew that I had to get up and move, or risk having my head rest in what was left of a plate of roast beef and mashed potatoes. The dance floor was calling. Jeff probably thought, from my eagerness, that I knew how to dance. He soon found out otherwise, but who cares when you are a little tipsy. (Yes, I am still a Christian.) I guess after all these years, there were still things we did not know about each other!

We danced and danced, along with fifty to sixty other couples in their forties and fifties. One thing I do need to mention is that NO self-respecting adult past the age of thirty-five, should be allowed to "fast dance" in public. After a while of sweating to the oldies, with the oldies, we took our seats and became entertained observers. It was comical and embarrassing to realize that we had been out there looking just as silly! Note to Old people: Slow dancing is acceptable and Ballroom dancing is especially acceptable, but fast dancing...not so much! I just hoped that no one had a video camera! This was the kind of stuff that finds its way to "You Tube".

Now that I was wide awake and duly entertained, we sat, and we sipped. Our very generous friend never let my glass get empty. I was not a partier or a drinker, so I was not really paying attention to my alcohol intake. A few sips here, a few sips there, here a sip there a sip...I did not think I was feeling any effect from the wine (silly me) and I was having a great time.

It was almost midnight. Our friends ordered a bottle of champagne and we prepared to toast in the New Year. We stood up for the countdown, kazoo blowing and glass clinking. I looked at Jeff and said "OH, I think I'm feeling dizzy". Five, Four, Three, Two, One ...HAPPY NEW YEAR!!

New Year wishes, clinking glasses, kisses and hugs. It was all exciting. Jeff said to me, "Drink your champagne sweetie". So, I did. A big gulp! Just a side note here: I like a lot of ice in my drinks, so unlike most people, I had ice in my champagne, and I sucked a piece of ice into my mouth. Even in my wine induced haze, I noticed Jeff and our friends were all looking at me with rather horrified expression, on their faces. It slowly dawned on me that perhaps this was not ice in my mouth. Much to everyone's obvious sighs of relief, I quickly retrieved a beautiful diamond ring from the tip of my tongue. My knight proposed to me, right there, on the spot amid all the hoopla.

Life as I knew it would never be the same.

5

The Honeymoon

We decided to get married in March. It was a short engagement, but we had known each other for many years, it seemed, and we were not getting any younger. Our plan was to grow old together and at our age, the odds of celebrating milestone anniversaries are not quite as good as we might like to think. We had a lot of living to cram into whatever time we would have together!

We decided to get married on a cruise ship. It would be a "Win Win" situation. We could get married on the cruise ship, we could have our families with us enjoying a great vacation and we could honeymoon all at the same time. This would be the perfect venue.

I began Googling cruises and collecting travel information. We called Jeff's best friend, Dwight, to see if he could go with us and perform our marriage ceremony on the ship. All the plans were falling into place, the reservations were verified, and a flurry of activity ensued.

The cruise was to depart from Miami, Florida on a Sunday. We all agreed that we should arrive in Miami on Saturday. That way we would not have to worry about traffic or any other unforeseen issues along the way that might keep us from boarding the ship on time. My parents decided to fly and graciously took my youngest son with them. My middle child also elected to fly and coordinated his own travel plans. He would meet up with his grandparents and younger brother at the airport, and then the four of them would be picked up by my brother and his spouse, who had driven down to Florida a few days earlier. Everyone would stay in a hotel on Saturday night and then depart for the Port of Miami, less than 15 miles away, on Sunday morning. Dwight and his entourage elected to fly and were coming in on Saturday evening, as well. Our best friends, also flying, were not coming until early Sunday morning. Although I was anxious about their Sunday morning arrangement, they had to leave two little ones behind with relatives and wanted to minimize their time away. I completely understood. I had my children with me, thus alleviating all chances of guilty mommy syndrome.

Unfortunately, after paying for seven cruise tickets, we could not afford to fly. I had an eight-passenger van that was relatively comfortable and in good repair. We even did our due diligence and had it serviced prior to the trip.

Late on Friday afternoon, Jeff and I along with my oldest son and his girlfriend, hit the road. Our first stop was Winston Salem, North Carolina, where we picked up Jeff's mother and stepfather. We arrived at their place around 10:00 pm, had a bite to eat and grabbed some shuteye, for the night. Rising bright and early the next morning, we quickly ate breakfast and then piled into the van for the remaining leg of the trip. Twelve hours to go.

We arrived at the hotel on Saturday afternoon where Jeff's brother David, soon joined us. The hotel personnel advised us that they would be running a shuttle to the Port of Miami beginning at 10:00 a.m. Sunday morning and we were welcome to leave our vehicle in the hotel parking lot, for $5.00 a day.

My parents, son and brother had also arrived and were checked in at a different hotel. We were now all in Florida, except for our friends flying in on Sunday. More importantly, we were all less than 15 minutes from the Port of Miami. Big sigh of relief!

It should have been simple, from there on out. We had planned and planned. We had tried to think of everything. But, as my (now) husband often says, "No good deed goes unpunished" and now we can add "No good plan goes unspoiled".

We awoke early the next morning, anticipating our first day on board the cruise ship "Victory". We collected our luggage and walked to the shuttle spot designated by the hotel desk clerk. There would be eleven of us. As we rounded the corner, we saw an exceptionally large group of people standing around, also waiting for the shuttle. No problem, I thought, we will have plenty of room on the bus for everyone and their luggage.

Silly, silly me!

6

The Saga Begins

Obstacle number one:

It was not a bus. It was a minivan! ONE small minivan! There had to be at least 40 people waiting for a ride. This was NOT going to work. Time was of the essence here. We had to be on the ship, at the very latest, by 2:00 p.m.. Boarding started at 11:00 a.m.. So, we put our heads together and decided to use our own van and park in the extended parking lot at the Port of Miami. It would be $10.00 a day, but we had 11 people to split it between. This was probably a better idea anyway. So, group number one, (Jeff's mom and stepfather, Dwight and his spouse, their two friends, Jeff and I) piled in the van. Smooth sailing, right up to the luggage drop. We put our luggage on the tractor pulled trailers and everybody, except for me, proceeded to boarding. I wanted to wait for Jeff so I would board with the second group. First mission accomplished: Group number one has been deposited and is boarding!

Off drove my husband-to-be, to pick up group number two.

Although it was early March, the temperature was hovering in the high 80's, so I found some shade and sat on the curb to wait for the second half of our group. It took us fifteen minutes to get to the port, fifteen minutes to get back to the hotel and then fifteen minutes back to the port again. In about 50 minutes with no second group in sight, I was beginning to worry. Where were they?

Then, my cell phone rang.

Obstacle number two:

Our van had broken down somewhere on the interstate. Jeff called me to get the number for AAA Towing Service. Apparently, he had left his wallet with his luggage, which was with the second group waiting to be picked up.

Upon speaking with AAA, he learned it would be approximately 2 hours before they would be able to come to assist. He explained that he was supposed to be boarding a cruise ship and he really needed them to hurry. In the meantime, he wanted me to call the remaining group and tell them to get on the hotel shuttle, NOW! He needed them to make sure they brought his luggage with them and to be sure to get his passport and wallet out of his luggage before it was checked in. So, I called and frantically relayed the unfolding events and told them to catch the next shuttle. Unfortunately, the hotel shuttle had stopped running and there was only one option now, a Taxi.

The second group arrived. I saw them crossing the parking lot and trotted off to meet them. "Where is Jeff's luggage?" I asked. They pointed to an 8' x 10' trailer, loaded about 10 feet high with luggage. It was being pulled away by a tractor. "Aaaahhhhh", Jeff would not be able to board the ship without his passport! I started running after that trailer.

Meanwhile, Jeff had managed to get the van started, and was heading toward the port. Remember that old song from "Hee Haw"? "...if it were not for bad luck, I'd have no luck at all. Glooooommmmm, despair and agony on me." That is about what Jeff was feeling when the van broke down the *second time*! This time there would be no restarting it AND because he had moved, AAA could not find him. He called them again to let them he was about a mile further up the road from where he had been previously. When they finally found him, there was no time to take the van to a service station, so he asked them to tow it to the Port of Miami parking garage. He did not have his AAA card or any cash with him, because I had his wallet with me. Just to make things a tad bit more stressful, his cell phone battery was almost dead.

Obstacle number three:

Meanwhile back to boarding the ship; everyone is onboard except two of my children, one of their girlfriends, Jeff and me. Those that knew what was going on with the vehicle escapade were instructed not to mention it to any of our parents, all of whom were already onboard the ship. My kids wanted to wait with me, but I told them to go ahead and board. It was 1:00 p.m. already and cut off time was 2:00 p.m.. I sat back down on the curb, getting more stressed with each passing minute, trying not to cry. I looked around to make sure the children were on the ship and to my surprise they were headed back toward me. It seemed that because the girlfriend, was a minor (17 years old), they would not let her board without me. This was ridiculously insane to me. After all, they were going to let my children on without me, one of which was also 17 years old! What to do, what to do? I was getting a little frazzled.

My seventeen-year-old son says "Hey mom, why don't we just try to get in through a different line? The worst that can happen is that they say no, again." So, they did and in they got! Thank God for small miracles and minor obstacles!

Obstacle number four:

Jeff calls again. He has been picked up by a non-English speaking tow truck driver who does not know where the Port of Miami is. WHAT?! It must be one of the biggest things in

Miami!!! The driver is talking to Jeff through the dispatcher on the CB radio. Jeff needs me to get an address for the Port of Miami. I looked at the front of the building and saw no indication of an address. (Jeff is now down to one battery bar on his cell phone.) I dashed inside the terminal and asked the customer service person what the address was. He did not know. OH MY GOSH!!! I could not believe it. There were two of them, and neither one knew the address of the place they worked! I explained to them that my finance' was currently in a tow truck somewhere and it was now 1:45 p.m.. They were kind enough to tell me that since they knew about our situation, they would let us board as late as 2:30 p.m.. I raced back outside, called Jeff back and as I was about to burst into tears, looked up and saw the address printed across the glass, twenty feet up, at the very top of the terminal. Who looks that high up for an address?? Sheesh!

Obstacle number five:

When will it end?! I still had not cried, but I had been close to tears several times. I thought I was doing rather well. I sat back down on the curb to wait. I started to think of alternate plans. If we missed the ship, we could stay in Miami for the night and then fly to Puerto Rico and board the ship there. Of course, our luggage would have gone without us, but that would be only a minor issue. I had my backpack with me. It contained medications, hats, books and thankfully a bottle of SPF 30 sun lotion. Jeff called me one last time and said there was only one parking lot at the Port of Miami that could handle a towed vehicle. I would have to meet him at the parking lot attendant's booth to pay the lot fee because, as mentioned earlier, I had his wallet. "Lot G will be on the left," he said. "Just keep walking until you find it".

Did I mention that I was wearing flip flops, carrying a 20 lb. backpack and that it was quite hot? I started walking. And I walked and I walked. Thinking I must have missed it, I stopped and asked some employees I saw, working on a loading dock, where Lot G was. Predictably, they had no idea. So, I kept walking. Just as I was about to give up, I saw Jeff and the tow truck. Thank you, Jesus! We paid the tow truck driver and speed walked back to the terminal. We got there with only minutes to spare. All other passengers were already onboard, so we walked directly up the boarding plank and onto the ship.

That should have been enough excitement for one day, but there was more to come. We walked onto the ship and there before me were more than a thousand people all milling around on the main deck. Okay, okay, probably not a thousand, but I do not like crowds. All I knew was that there were a LOT of people in one small place. I was already stressed to the breaking point and struggling to hold back the tears. Now I was in "ship shock". Having never been on a cruise ship before, I had no idea what to expect. Jeff steered me to the bar for a quick drink (yes, I am still a Christian) and then we headed to our cabin. I needed some time to de-stress. I had just managed to quell a small panic attack, when they announced that before embarkation, we would be having a lifeboat drill. No problem, I could handle that. Since my fiancé and I were registered in two different rooms, pending our marriage, we were not in the same lifeboat section. I took my life jacket out of the closet and headed to the muster station. How bad could this be? If you have ever been on a cruise ship, you already know the answer to that question. They line you up, side by side, four rows deep. It was hot and we were required to actually put on the life jackets. Some of the passengers had been on the ship since ten or eleven o'clock that morning. They were now drunk and not the least bit interested in coming to muster for lifeboat instructions. So, packed together like taquitos in a casserole dish, we waited and prayed for a breeze. We waited and we waited for our drunken shipmates to grace us with their presence. It had become clear that the rest of us would be held hostage until all passengers were accounted for. When the crew was certain everyone was there, twenty long, humid, hot minutes later, they briefed us on emergency lifeboat instructions and released us to our cabins.

Finally, we set sail. Jeff's room, the one we would share, had a balcony. Most of our gang went there to watch us pull away from the dock. We were rewarded with a spectacular view of Miami Beach and a stunning skyline. Everything seemed to be going smoothly.

I guess it was because I finally had time to relax and reflect on the past eight hours that I found myself laying on the bed, with a stomach-ache, sobbing. Darn these nerves. My poor Jeff did not know what to do, so he did what most men in this situation would do... he called my mother. Of course she came right away and soothed my frayed nerves. No matter what age we are, we never get too old for the soothing arms of our mothers. Everything is going to be okay, deep breaths, in and out, all is well now...or so I thought.

7

Getting Married

We planned to have our marriage ceremony, first thing the next morning, at the bow of the ship on the upper most deck. We woke up from a wonderfully comfortable, peaceful night of rest to a cloudy, rainy day. It rained all morning. It rained all afternoon. It rained all evening. At times, it tapered off to a mist, but the wind was blowing at about 25 mph!

It was time for Plan B. Jeff talked to the ship director and successfully reserved us a small room for the ceremony. Turned out the small room was a lovely Piano Bar. All ministers should get married in a Piano Bar. It makes for a fun story when people ask where you got married. The setting was quite nice. The actual piano was circled by a counter that had ivory piano keys all the way around the top of it. The carpet was black and dotted with exceptionally large, very bright, green Shamrocks. Ah yes, this was not just any bar, it was an IRISH Piano Bar. My kids loved it. At this point, I did not really care where we got married. I just wanted it done!!!

For the ceremony, I had purchased a knee length cream colored dressed that had a slight "v" shape in the front hemline and a sheer ruffle flowing down from the waistline. The one-inch shoulder straps were also sheer and blended into a sweetheart neckline with a splattering of sequins. I had purchased a matching faux diamond necklace and earring set to complete the ensemble. I had also purchased some uncomfortable shoes to wear. Unfortunately, I have fat feet and that was even before I was fat!

Now that the Piano Bar was secured and we knew that we were not going to have to use Plan C, (which was get married in Jeff's cabin), I rushed to my cabin to get into my beautiful dress. We were finally going to get married. I put on my dress and primped in front of the mirror, making sure nothing was out of place. It was then that I noticed that you could see panty lines right through the thin fabric! YES, I did try it on in the store, but I had failed to notice this slightly embarrassing detail. I must have had stars in my eyes, or maybe the lighting was weird. Thank goodness I had had the foresight to pack white under garments. There was nothing I could do about the lines now, unless I opted to go commando... It was just a fleeting thought. "Oh well I thought, perhaps no one will notice."

As it turned out, it was only half as embarrassing as I had anticipated, because most of the men were looking at a continuing parade of breasts and I am not talking chicken. When it comes to breast, if they are not hanging down to your belly button, men will look at them. There were a lot of pretty girls in low cut dresses on this ship, so there was plenty for the eyes to consume. It dawned on me that it was probably only the ladies who were noticing my ghastly panty lines.

We made our way to the Piano Bar and took our places. Our best friends, Tom & Lindsay, stood up with us and Dwight performed our ceremony.

I cried. There does seem to be a pattern here, but I promise, they were tears of joy this time.

Our cruise was beautiful. The food was fabulous. The bed linens were lush. The balcony outside our cabin was enchanting and my new husband was perfect! Nothing could upset me now.

Well...maybe one more little thing. I had talked to the children about never going anywhere by themselves. The Buddy System never grows old. The youngest was thirteen, so they were old enough to explore the ship by themselves, but whenever we were to be in port, I was adamant that they should stay together. We would be in strange territory, on islands unknown to us, with customs we were not familiar with.

On the third day, we arrived at our first port in Puerto Rico. We were all in line to disembark, along with hundreds of other passengers. There were 19 of us and for the most part we were filing out onto the dock together or at least within seeing distance of each other. As we began to walk the long concrete docking area, the crowd started to thin out a little. I was trying to watch my kids and take in my surroundings all at the same time. Suddenly I realized that I did not see my youngest son. "Where's Andrew?" I asked. Everybody kind of looked around and then back at me. "Where's Andrew?! I asked again, in a much louder voice. Too late! A wave of panic was upon me. Everybody started hollering up the dock to the rest of our group that had gone ahead of us. I however had already dissolved into the beginning stages of hysteria, tears spilling down my face (yes again) while declaring "Oh My Gosh! I have lost my child in Puerto Rico!"

It seemed like a long time, but it was probably less than a minute before he was running back to me, apologizing and holding me in a big bear hug. "Mom, I was with David (Jeff's brother). Everything is okay. I'm sorry I scared you."

Everybody calmed down, everybody meaning ME, and we scattered about the island. As I walked, I wondered if Jeff was starting to wonder what he had gotten himself into. Did he know I was a blubbering idiot? I am sure not, but he did say for "better or worse". For that matter he said, "in sickness and health", too. He had no idea what was to come.

The rest of the cruise was wonderful and uneventful as far as nerves are concerned. The islands were just like the pictures. The Caribbean waters were gorgeous, and I got to snorkel for the very first time. I was not quite comfortable with the scuba mask on my face, but Andrew stuck with me, coaxed me out into the very cold water and showed me how to breathe through the snorkel. Once I got the hang of it, I loved it! There were so many species of colorful fish. Yellow ones, orange ones, blue ones and stripped ones, big ones and small ones. Corals and sponges. I even saw starfish, real live starfish, lying on the rippled sandy ocean floor, just like in pictures! What an amazing adventure this cruise was.

We had an amazing honeymoon and were blessed to be able to share it with our family and friends.

8

One Day A Week

What exactly does a Christian minister do? (Warning, sarcasm alert.) Really, does anyone ever see them working except for those *mere* 4 hours on Sunday morning? What a life! Who would not love to work *only* on Sunday? Okay, so maybe you would not get the whole weekend off, but that is a small price to pay for having off Monday through Saturday. Ministers live a life of leisure; working just a few hours, seldom in their offices, often found napping and even living in free houses. They can leisurely read a book, catch an afternoon movie or go to the grocery store when it is not crowded.

Ministers are frequently seen at football, basketball, soccer and baseball games, house warming's, graduations, baptism parties and wedding receptions, where, of course, the food is always free. They are often invited to dinner and they regularly go to lunch with a group of people after church services on Sunday afternoon.

It has been said that people give ministers expensive gifts like used cars, nice clothes and shoes, computers, household items, lawn equipment, and the list goes on and on. Sounds like a great job. Those are some awesome perks. What other kind of job could you have that would measure up to all that? Ministers are living the life!

That is what a lot of people believe. Well, I am here to tell you that I personally know that this is not even close to being true! I now have the inside scoop. As a ministers' wife, I have seen things I did not want to see. Things I hope to never see again. I have been burdened with keeping secrets that I never wanted to know. Ministers see people at their best and at their worst and just when they think they have heard and seen it all, I can only say... Oh My Gosh! There is always something more bizarre and shocking than the last.

I do not know about all ministers, but after living with one and meeting and talking to a few others, I have found that they are, most likely, the busiest people you will ever meet. *Successful* ministers are living the life of frantic men and women, caught up in a demanding chaotic whirlpool of obligations. They are racing about like little army ants, carrying the weight of the world on their shoulders. They are on call twenty-four hours a day, seven days a week.

Yes, they are generally in a great mood, mostly jovial, always glad to see you and never too busy for a chat. However, underneath all of that is a sometimes overworked, harried person just trying to survive. Ministers are masters at covering and hiding their emotions and their own turmoil filled lives.

9

The Men and Women That Nourish Our Spiritual Health

All people have flaws, whether it be physical, mental, spiritual or some type of personality trait that is a little outside the norm of society. One of my husband's weakness is not using the word "NO". He tries desperately to make everyone happy.

Unfortunately, some people just do not seem to want to be happy. And sometimes saying "NO" is a necessary response.

Another thing: he is only one person! He really *cannot* be in two different meetings at the same time. And why do people expect him to be at the church EVERY night of the week and then declare that he only works on Sunday's? I know, I know...that is what I once thought, also.

Now, back to those perks I mentioned. You know the ones that I thought were so enticing? Well, come to find out, the four or five hours that most people think a minister works in a week, can be anywhere from forty to sixty hours. My husband is on call 24 hours a day, seven days a week. And because the sick and dying do not choose their time, he is even on call when he is on vacation. The only time he is *not* on call is when we are in the middle of the ocean without telephone service or any other means of communication. This is one of the reasons I love to go on cruises. My husband can actually relax!

Remember all those dinners and lunches I spoke of? Ninety percent of the time, we pick up the tab. My husband likes to take perspective new members and regular church members to lunch after church. He feels that it is a good way to get to know them better.

There was also the part where I mentioned reading a lot of books. Most of them are for research or personal growth so that he will be better prepared to help other people. Oh...and he taught himself to speed read, so he gets to read novels, as well.

The seemingly extracurricular activities that I talked about, i.e., soccer games, baseball games and football games, house warmings, weddings and graduations, they never stop! We rarely have a free night.

My husband is committed to his parishioners, young and old. He wants them all to know that he cares about them, so we attend events that are important to **them**.

Saturdays are a workday for Jeff. It took me a while to understand this. "Why can't you take off on Saturday, like everyone else?" I would ask.

The answer: Weekends are when most people are home from their daily jobs. That is why most of our Saturdays are spent attending function after function, often two or three in one day. If we do not have any middle or high school events to attend, then he will catch up on home visits.

I finally did get used to his(us) working weekends and I finally did get used to the fact that we could not take weekend vacations. (Although I have gotten used to it, I am not happy about it.)

Ministers can adapt to any situation while being compassionate and nurturing. Most of all they have learned to laugh at themselves and the situations that they find themselves in. They have learned to fly through the day by the seat of their pants/skirt, rocket out of bed in response to a ringing telephone and change clothes on the way out the door. They are crisis counselors and your best friend. They answer to a calling only they know and when they are tired and worn out, they keep on going. I am sure that God must have a sense of humor. I know that he gives these men and women the strength to go on and for that, we are all truly blessed.

As clergy spouses, we to have learned to improvise at the drop of a hat. We are ready to have people over for dinner at a moments' notice, or perhaps have a guest stay in our spare bedroom. We accompany our minister spouses on hospital visits, nursing home visits and parishioner home visits. We also go to weddings and funerals of people we do not even know.

Occasionally, we have to become like mamma & poppa bears protecting our cubs, but do not misunderstand, ministers are not weak individuals. They are highly capable of taking care of everybody and everything...except themselves! Everyone else comes first. They have no time for themselves and sometimes, unfortunately, their own family.

10

Learning to be a Minister's Wife

The Honeymoon was over and together, we began a new chapter in our lives as Mr. & Mrs. My husband tried to warn me that things would be different for me now that I was a minister's spouse. I thought I was prepared. I was not.

Now that I am his wife, I know exactly what being married to a minister means and I am here to tell you that any bizarre stories that you may have heard, they are probably true.

I found that I now had not just a new name, but a new identity, as well. Overnight, I had ceased being "me". I had now become "The Minister's Wife".

I did not have any qualms about being the spouse of a minister, but that was before I knew what was in store for us, or rather, I should say, ME! I might have had a few reservations if I had truly known what it would be like. I might have asked more questions and been a little better prepared.

This was Jeff's chosen lot in life, and he had been living it for many years. In all fairness, he did try to warn me. I love this man with all my heart, but it has been difficult at times. I have had to change some of my ways. I currently have a smile on my face. I must smile at everybody even when I do not feel like it. I cannot tell people what I really think, because I am "an extension of my husband". I have an image to uphold. His!

It is Jeff's belief that he needs to make *everyone* happy. He must be available twenty-four hours a day. If someone is upset or angry with him, he feels that he has failed them, in some way or another. I on the other hand, realize that making every-one happy is not even a remote possibility. Some people do not want to be happy. I cannot be bothered with their attitudes. More than once I have said to my husband, "I don't care what they think"! A wise man (my dad) once told me that when it comes to what people think, that I needed to care a little bit more and Jeff needed to care a little bit less. I do sound a little bit like the bad guy that does not care about people, but that is not the case at all. As you will see in the following pages, Min-isters have a tough road to hoe and it is the spouses that pull them through. It is the spouses that pick up the pieces of their husband's heart. It is the spouses that help them put life into perspective.

"Ministerhood", as I like to call it, is a way of life that can be both joyful and depressing, but one thing that is always true, it is NOT boring! The Minister's family is usually referred to as "the minister's spouse, the parsonage family, or the minister's kids". There are many times when I do not even get introduced by my name. i.e. "This is our minister's wife." To which I add, "Hi, I'm Karen".

As ministerial families we can be quite transient. Here one year and gone the next, or so it seems. Some ministers fortunately stay put in a church for at least a few years. We have had mostly long stays. However, because of the constant transitioning, many clerical families do not form close relationships with the parishioners of their churches. I learned from my new husband that during his seminary years, the ministers were advised to steer clear of close relationships with their parishioners. There are some legitimate reasons for this, but I am not sure I agree with them. We have made many friends over the years and yes sometimes it does get painful when we move on, but the deep friendships that we nurture, that survive our moves, far outweigh any pain.

The most difficult thing for me, as a minister's wife, are the social functions that I am required to attend. Spouses are expected to attend meetings, fellowship events and men's or women's groups. Some are expected to help in the kitchen with dinners, help with rummage and bake sales, help with fish frys and breakfast meetings. We attend bible studies, car washes, special events and whatever else comes along. I guess I should not say that we are actually required to attend all of these events; it just *feels* like we are. Even if we do not participate in an event, we will still make an appearance. My husband thinks that if we do not attend a function that someone's feelings may be hurt. He has this idea that he needs to be amongst his parishioners, wherever they are. Since he and I are "one" in God's eyes (and ours, too for that matter), I should be with him all the time. I can understand his feelings, but I often, quietly or NOT so quietly mutter, "This is NOT my job, it's YOURS!"

Being married to MY minister has put me in a much broader social circle. My husband is an over the top extrovert. I am his opposite! I am basically a wallflower kind of person. I do not like to be noticed and I am uncomfortable at large social functions. I am not antisocial, but I am definitely much more comfortable in small groups of people, preferably ones that I know. At large functions, I feel awkward. I do not know what to do with myself. People do not want to tell me what to do because I am "The Minister's Wife", so I just stand around and smile a lot. How embarrassing is that?! However, you will not know that I am uncomfortable or embarrassed. My face will not turn red. I will not quake in my shoes. I have mastered being a good faker. I have learned to hide my emotions almost as well as my spouse has. I can smile while holding back tears of frustration. I can carry on conversations about nothing and I can go from person to person, making *them* feel at ease. Why? Because that is MY job. Do not take that statement the wrong way. I LOVE my church family. Each and every one of them! I am just saying that I have gotten to know them by taking myself out of my comfort zone. If I were not the minister's wife, I would not have gotten to know them and experience the blessings that so many have brought to my life! Being outside of my comfort zone has been good for me and has made it possible for me to meet and form relationships with some great people. God always knows what he is doing!

In some respects, being a ministerial family is like being in the military. We never know when or where we might be assigned to next. Our lives are not our own. Very simply put, our minister spouse and thus we, are governed by the church. The job comes first. Unfortunately, ministers do not get recognized for their service. Although they do not serve their country through the armed services, they do serve their country's people and their needs, selflessly giving of themselves while sharing God's love. And like the military, they do not just serve their homeland. Some are called by God to go to other countries, to show and share God's love through mission trips or by helping natural disaster victims affected by floods, earthquakes, tornadoes and hurricanes.

I just have to pray that wherever the church sends us, it is where God wants us to be. Wherever it is, we will go and serve graciously. Yet, I still sometimes wonder if we really are where God wants us to be. I pray and listen for direction, but I do not know if I hear the voice of God or if it is my sub-conscience. Maybe my sub-conscience IS the voice of God. The fact is, I am afraid to hear the voice of God. What if he tells me to do something I do not want to do? Or go somewhere I do not want to go? What if I am not smart enough? I like it here safe and secure in my little corner of the United States. I just know if I pray and ask God to send me where he would have me serve that I might end up in Zimbabwe or Ethiopia! I think he wants us to reach people that may be unlike ourselves. Perhaps someone physically or mentally damaged, someone who is down on their luck or maybe a young person heading down the wrong path in life. Maybe a well to do person who thinks they do not need God in their life. Only God knows where he needs us to be and he will ultimately lead us to wherever that is.

I am sure that there are more than a few ministers that just show up on Sunday morning. They do not visit or engage in the lives of their parishioners. There are not invested in the church that they are serving. Not all ministers are called by God and not all minister's spouses are led by their faith. It is also a certainty that not all spouses will support their minister's chosen path. What is evident though is that behind every successful minister, called by God, is a faithful and loving spouse or support system that will encourage, listen to and help him or her in whatever way they can.

11

THE PEDESTAL

The dreaded pedestal. There is another thing that I feel compelled to share and that is the personal, physical, mental and spiritual standard to which ministers are held. Not just by their own families, like most people, but by their parishioners, as well. Intentionally and unintentionally, people, churched and non-churched, put ministers up on a pedestal. Ministers really are not thought of as "normal" human beings. I know that seems like a ridiculous statement but stick with me for a bit and I think you will agree.

The minister's life is on constant display. They are not supposed to make mistakes (sin). They are not supposed to say curse words or have a grumpy day. They are not supposed to drink alcohol and certainly never step foot in a bar. They should never get a speeding ticket or, heaven forbid, a reckless driving ticket.

They are expected to have perfect kids and perfect spouses. They are expected to be always dressed modestly (no tank tops in public). People expect them to be strong in the wake of a disaster, both personal and worldly. They must always "hold it together".

It is a precarious perch to be on. The men and women of faith walking this earth and trying to save souls for our God, are a strong bunch of human beings. However, not even they could withstand all that they go through, in their ministry, without the divine guidance of God the Father.

12

DON'T ASK / DON'T TELL

Do not ask / Do not tell; These words have become a rule in my new life. I sometimes have the inside scoop on other people's lives, like it or not. I thought I would like to be "in the know" but have found that it isn't all it's cracked up to be! When you are "in the know", you are burdened with keeping secrets that you never wanted to know in the first place. I have become acutely aware of what I can only describe as an invisible shield, that we all hide behind. Sometimes the shield masquerades as a mask that hides emotions. Or it could be a medication that alters one's personality or perhaps a closed door that hides bad habits. Only God knows who we truly are and only he knows our innermost thoughts, deeds and misdeeds.

What I have learned is that people have two faces. A *good* face and an *ugly* face; the good face is the one that we let everybody see, the one that we try to keep in the forefront. It is the one we wear out to dinner or to church, to work or shopping. It is our public face.

Then there is the ugly face. The people most likely to see this face are usually those closest to us, i.e., our parents, spouse, children and siblings. The usual exception to this is a person's doctor or minister. That mean, spiteful, unkind face can rear its ugliness at any time, and without warning. We have all experienced it!

The scary thing is that you cannot tell from looking at someone's face which face you are about to deal with. You must first engage. I have seen a person go from good to ugly in a matter of seconds, right before my scared, shocked or teary eyes. I have seen glimpses of peoples' "other" selves and what I have observed is not always pretty. I have heard things and seen things that I never wanted to hear or see. I know things that I cannot talk about. In fact, anything my husband may have shared with me is non-repeatable. All inside information stops here, in my head, right between my ears.

I can only imagine the turmoil that my husband goes through on a weekly basis. He and other ministers "see all and hear all". They deal with people when they are at their best and when they are at their worst. Just when they think they have heard and seen it all, I can only say OMGosh! There is always something more bizarre and/or shocking than the last.

Eventually, most ministers will at some point, go through a rough patch in their ministry. They begin to tire both mentally and physically. Their pastoral and personal burdens can become overwhelming. Many ministers feel that if they have not been able to "fix" everybody and everything, then they are incompetent and unworthy.

Depression is not an uncommon malady for ministers, but to the secular observer it is not something they expect their minister to experience. After all, their minister *is* the counselor, and he/she has a direct line to God, right? They are not supposed to be affected by the hateful and hurtful things that people say.

In response to this expectation, real **or** imagined, the minister feels that they must not appear to be anything but perfect, hence they fight to maintain their precarious perch on that ridiculous pedestal.

So, the ultimate question is this; Who helps the depressed, sad, inconsolable minister? Who visits with them? Who lifts them up? Who helps them get back on track?

Who nurtures their mental health?

13

PARSONAGE PATTER

Many Methodist ministers from the late 1700's through the 1800's, were known as Circuit Riders. The clergy would be assigned a particular *area* or *circuit*, also referred to as a "charge". A pastor would be appointed to the charge by his bishop. During the year, the acting pastor was expected to visit each church on the charge at least once, and possibly start some new ones. The circuit was demanding on those who undertook this grueling ministry, and many died before the age of forty.

Other ministers chose to stay in more hospitable surroundings. The people of a community church would pull together and purchase a home for the minister to reside in, which is traditionally known as a parsonage. Since the ministers, most of whom were bachelors, were appointed on a yearly basis, these men moved from place to place with little more than the clothes on their backs, their books and study materials. They were typically poor and had very few personal belongings. Most communities were unable to pay the minister, so the church community would not only provide him a home to live in, but also the minimal provisions that he would require. The parsonage furnishings usually included the essentials, such as a bed, a table, a writing desk, a pot and eating utensils. Some parsonages might also be adorned with curtains and bed linens that had been hand crafted by the community women.

It was not uncommon for the minister to be paid with eggs, grains or meats. Although tasty, these gifts of food did not help pay the heating bills. Due to drafty homes, bitter winters and a lack of proper heating, it was not unheard of for a minister to freeze to death in his home. As a result, the church began to provide some sort of heating source during the winter months.

Thankfully, this tradition of necessities and personal comforts have changed over the years.

Today, most ministers are married and have families. Also, women have joined the ministerial ranks, bringing with them their own set of needs. Even though much has changed over the years, there are still lingering traditions that have been hard to overcome. In the not so distant past, there were people of the church, usually the governing body, who thought that since the parsonage belonged to the church, the minister and his family should live by the church committee's standards. The appointed church committee would decorate and hang curtains and pictures of their own liking, assuming that the incoming family did not want, have or need any personal items in their homes. Depending on the financial status of the church, the parsonage might be in an upper class, middle class or lower-class neighborhood. The family had no say in what was or was not to be in the already furnished parsonage. A parsonage was not really a minister's home. It was just a place to live. Personal tastes were basically non-existent.

Since ministerial families do not know the ins and outs of where they are going to live and who they will be dealing with, a move can be and *is* stressful. In our first parsonage together, my husband arrived at our new residence while I was at work. He was taking pictures of the furniture, curtains, wall decorations, etc. and sending them to me, via text message. I was aghast to see a very peach colored, floral and bird print couch. Yes, I said birds!! As is most parsonage furniture, this couch had been passed down and now we were to be blessed with it. Some of the women on the parsonage committee were quite happy with this piece of furniture. In fact, they liked it so much that they had purchased a brand-new peach plaid couch to go with it. Now really, think about this. When is the last time you saw a peach couch in a furniture store? At first, I cried (it was a hormone thing!) because I knew I had to live with it. My husband did not want to hurt anyone's feelings by moving it to the attic. He told me I should at least keep it in the living room until after Christmas. When I finished crying, I took a deep breath and said to myself, "Self, you can handle this". And so, I would!

Also, on this move-in day, my husband sent me an e-mail picture of a huge flower picture that someone had purchased especially to be mounted over the fireplace. It was a pretty picture, but again it was not my taste. I had a very pretty, long rectangular shaped, framed mirror that I had specifically purchased, years earlier, to hang over my fireplace. Knowing that I was already upset about the couch and apt to burst into tears at any moment, my husband was treading lightly. "This is going to be *my* home! I want *my* things." He gently suggested that we hang it in another room of the house. We did, it looked nice and my mirror won its spot above the mantle. Small victory for me! Yea!

After a few days of the couches "growing" on me, I got used to the new peach plaid one. It was not what I would have picked out, but it was a genuinely nice couch. The other one however, was a different story. It was still ugly. Some of our friends thought it was awful and others really liked it. However, it would not have mattered to me if the whole world liked it, it was just NOT "me"! Soon thereafter, I dubbed the couch "The Angry Bird Couch". Reason being, the blue birds that were all over the couch had eyes that were shaped like tiny slits. They were angry eyes. So much for blue birds of happiness!

As dramatic as these experiences were to me, I knew that there were other families going through their own "moving hell" on the exact same day as me.

One of our friends, who had been in the ministry much longer than us, told of a time when the minister and his family did not see or know anything about their new residence until they arrived, curbside, with the moving truck. The expected procedure was that there was to be a three-hour window in which one family moved out and the next family moved in. This system ensured that the church was never without a minister for more than three hours. Unfortunately, this left virtually no time for the current occupants to clean the house after they moved their belongings out. It felt like you were moving into a dirty hotel room, but on a larger scale. Yuck!

Often, the first few days in a new home were fraught with a frenzy of cleaning. Fortunately for me, the parsonages that I have moved into, were beautifully clean!

Move-in week was also the time for making note of any major repair issues, such as non-working appliances, missing fixtures or damaged walls.

Another friend told of a moving day in which they were sitting outside of their newly appointed residences with their children, pets and a moving truck full of possessions while the current family leisurely sat around the kitchen table eating lunch. They were supposed to be packed up and out of the house by noon. Unfortunately, this minister and his family seemed to be in no hurry and had not even finished packing up their belongings. When the new minister knocked on the door, he was told that they would finish moving their stuff out after they were done with their lunch! The new minister and his family had no choice but to sit in the hot car and wait. Of course, this meant that the kitchen was left in a mess.

This same friend also relayed a story about their children who had gone into their new residences and sat down on the parsonage provided couch. One of the children stuck their hand between the couch cushions and pulled out a half-eaten sandwich. The children thought it was amusing, but gross. The mother was appalled.

In another incident, upon arrival at their new home, the minister and his family entered the front door and immediately noticed that the home was in desperate need of a fresh coat of paint. The walls were dirty and dingy. To make matters worse, the foyer was adorned with an unattractive "horse-hair" couch. After cleaning the best that they could, they began to move in their own furniture. The distasteful "horsehair" couch was removed from the foyer. Soon thereafter, a visiting church member noticed that the couch had been moved to another area of the house. Apparently, this person had some sort of attachment to this piece of furniture and was not happy about its new location. They had no problem telling the minister that the couch should be put back where it *"belonged"*, in the foyer! They even tried to bargain it back into position by telling the minister that if it were returned to the foyer, they would agree to pay for the paint to re-paint the walls.

In yet another moving episode, the minister and his family were appointed to a church that was not in a particularly affluent area. Though this parsonage needed a lot of work, the congregation was not able to afford the cost to paint, upgrade or handle any kind of repair. The first evening they were there, the minister and his family sat down at the table to eat dinner. All of a sudden, they heard a creaking and cracking noise and the chair he was sitting in went straight through the floor, landing in the foundation crawl space. The startled minister was thankfully, unhurt. He hauled himself out of the hole and immediately placed a call to the church parsonage committee. In a short time, there was a knock at the door. A gentleman entered, carrying a large piece of plywood and a rug. The plywood was nailed over the hole and a rug was placed over it. When the family moved out years later, the plywood/rug "fix" remained in place.

Fortunately, these experiences are not the norm. Though most parsonages need updating they are usually found to be in decent condition and are in relatively nice neighborhoods.

I personally have lived in two very nice parsonages. The difference between owning or renting and living in a parsonage is this; If you own the house, you are responsible for repairs and upgrades. If you rent a house, you are not responsible for anything other than repairing what you damage. If you live in a parsonage, you are not responsible for either repairs or upgrades. However, you also cannot do repairs or upgrades without permission from the church committee. Anything you did not like (perhaps a hideous light fixture) that you wanted to replace, would have to be approved by a church committee. As a result, though not required, the parsonage family will do most repairs or changes themselves and simply store any replaced items so that they can be put back when the family moves.

14

A WORLD OF CHANGES

Changing jobs, changing houses, changing furniture, changing banks, changing subscriptions, changing pharmacies, changing doctors, changing veterinarians. Changing, changing, changing, everything changes. Some changes are good. Some are not.

Usually ministers move several times during their career. At the beginning of each year, our particular denomination of ministers is required to complete a form indicating their desire for their next appointment. The choices are;

Option 1. Desires to continue in their present appointment.

Option 2: Desires a move

Option 3 Desires a move but willing to continue in their current appointment.

As can be expected, many ministers struggle with making this decision. If they are not unhappy at their current location, the decision can be a difficult one to make. The minister can become comfortable with their role in their current church. They will have learned the personality of their current appointment, thus learning how to handle most situations that arise within this particular community of people. A move can mean a promotion to a larger church or it can be a step backwards.

My husband starts to get antsy at around five years. By the time seven years rolls around, if he has not moved yet, it is time. He likes the change and the challenge of a new appointment. He likes the opportunity to start over again. His feeling is that once he has brought a church as far as he can take it, then it is time for him to move on. A new minister with a different style and ideas can come in and take the church in a new direction, breathing new life, excitement and enthusiasm into the set routines that most fall into. On the flip side, the newly appointed minister may be too "different" from the previous minister and the appointment becomes a daily struggle for both the minister and the congregants.

When the time comes to complete the "form", my husband usually checks option three (Desires a move, but is willing to continue in the current appointment). Then, if the Bishop feels that he should move he does, and if not, then he stays at his currently appointed church. Thus far, my husband's churches have always asked him to stay. If he has decided that he is ready for a move, he will very carefully explain his reasons for checking option number three.

In theory, the system for orchestrating moves is a good system. However, as with any system, there can always be problems and this one is no exception. Sometimes a minister will check option two (desires a move) and then tell their congregants that the bishop is *making* them move. Unfortunately, this happens all too often. This happens when the minister wants to make a move but does not want the parishioners to think it was his choice. In this way, the church people do not feel like they are being abandoned and the minister can maintain a cordial and happy atmosphere all the way to end of his appointment.

Unfortunately, this scenario makes it more difficult for the new minister coming in. The seemingly "forced" move causes the church members to feel like the new minister is pushing out their beloved minister. This is obviously not the ideal situation for the new minister, who is sometimes met with "the cold shoulder" from misinformed parishioners.

Anyway... all that mess aside, let us talk about moving. It can be exciting, interesting, fun. Wait, no that would be an amusement park! I have appropriately titled the next section: Grrrrrrrr, the move.

15

GRRRRRRR... THE MOVE

Moves physically happen at the end of June. However, hopefully sometime in March, the minister will find out to which church and to where he/she will be moving. Here is how one of ours worked:

January (conversation between my husband and I):

"I put in for a move," He says.
"You did?" I reply.
"Yes, but I said I'd be willing to stay. I really want to move though, but I will stay if I have to."
I am relatively new to this, remember? So, I say "What does that mean? Are we moving or not?"
"Maybe. Most likely" He says.
"When will we know?" I ask.
"We'll probably know sometime in February or March. The District Superintendent will call and hopefully give me a couple of choices. We won't know anything until then."

"February or March? You've got to be kidding," I reply, while dramatically rolling my eyes. "So, our lives are in limbo until then?" I say.

"Kind of. If you think about it like that. But not really," He says.

My final response was, "HUH?"

In the days that followed, I started thinking that maybe I should begin getting rid of stuff and packing a few things, just in case. If we ended up *not* moving, at the very least, I would have cleaned out some junk!

February came and went. We started to talk about where we would be willing to move. My parents are older and currently lived only a mile away. I wanted to be able to get home in a hurry, if they were to need me. Also, as a cancer survivor, it was important to us that I not have to find a new oncology doctor. With all of this in mind, my husband decided to tell the District Superintendent (DS) that if we moved, we needed to be within two hours of where we were currently serving.

Now, all that was left to do was wait for the telephone call advising us of our options.

Also, my husband had been and was preparing for a mission trip to Haiti. He had felt a strong call to go to Haiti, soon after the devastating earthquake of 2008. He spoke with The United Methodist Committee On Reliefs (UMCOR) about taking a team of volunteers. He learned that in order to represent a UMC team, he would have to attend a Haiti training session that would be taking place in Georgia. Prior to taking a team himself, he would first have to go on a conference or district mission trip with leaders that had previously been there. Apparently, even a year later there were still a lot of logistical and political issues on the Haitian Island. Haiti also had restrictions on who could enter their country and what purpose they might have for being there.

After preparing and planning for a year, the time had finally come to go. He was on a conference team. The plane tickets had been purchased.

Coincidentally, at the same time, meetings and appointments started to fall into place regarding the upcoming minister relocations. The DS, who knew about and had approved my husband's trip, called to advise him that they would be calling him during their Cabinet Session on a particular day, to discuss his placement. As fate would have it, it was the same day that he would be flying to Haiti.

If he could not receive the phone call, he could end up serving anywhere in the state! Quite a scary thought for a seasoned minister! He did not want to take a pay cut and he did not want to end up in a little remote church somewhere out in the boonies. He started scrambling trying to find a cell phone that would work in Haiti. It was not an easy task, but he talked to some telephone technical people at a leading cellular company and got a new SIM card for his phone. He left for Haiti feeling confident that he would be able to communicate whenever necessary. Nevertheless, before leaving he gave me permission to make decisions for him.

Oh Great, I thought! Leave it up to ME to ruin his career. I was NOT happy.

He left for Haiti. The first night would be spent in Washington DC. The departing flight would be the following morning at 5:00 a.m. I sent him off with hugs and kisses, well wishes, warnings to not get kidnapped, contract malaria or dysentery AND to promise to come home safely.

Two days later:
"Mrs. Cannon, this is the secretary for the District Superintendent. We have been trying to get in touch with Rev. Cannon all morning regarding his appointment. We haven't been able to contact him."

To which I wanted to reply "DUH!" He told her he would be on an airplane bound for Haiti! But instead, I said "I will try to get in contact with him and have him call you as soon as he is available."

An hour later I received another call, this time from the DS herself.

"Tell Jeff to call me on my cell phone. I am in session, but it is imperative that I speak with him. I will have my cell phone in the meeting with me and I will answer it when he calls."

I tried his international cellular number about every fifteen minutes for the next three hours. By the time we finally connected he had gotten off the airplane, been through customs and was in route to Port Au Prince. He had realized that the international chip for his telephone was not working so he borrowed a telephone from one of the locals. He immediately called the DS on her cell phone AND as you probably guessed, she did not answer. Good Grief!! Well, it took him several more attempts and hours before he finally got through to her.

The option that they gave him was not what we would have liked. However, because we had specified that we wanted to stay in the area, his options were limited. Had we been willing to move anywhere in the state, he would have probably gotten a bigger church and a raise. But at this time in our lives the church's status and salary were not the most important factor for us.

We discussed for a few brief minutes and then decided that the church they were offering, which would result in an $8,000.00 pay cut, was probably the best move for us. It was not an easy decision. The reduction in salary was quite troublesome for my husband. He felt as if it was a step backwards and a slap in the face for a job well done. Every church he had served had flourished and grown under his leadership and yet he was being offered a church with a lower salary. We reasoned it out and realized that if we had been willing to move further away this probably would not have happened.

Location, health issues and my job played a part in the overall decision and although he would be receiving a lower salary it allowed us to stay in the area. This meant I would be able to keep my job, my doctors and be close to my family. I knew that my husband was making this sacrifice for me! Did I mention that he is my knight in shining armor?

On to the moving part: Traditionally, in our denomination, the church provides a house for the pastor and his family and a yearly housing cost is figured in as part of the pastor's salary. Also, certain rooms of the house are required to be furnished by the church.

The church provided furnishings include living room furniture, dining room furniture and kitchen furniture. Also, if there are more than 3 bedrooms in the house, the church will provide furniture for the fourth. This means that furniture is passed from ministerial family to ministerial family for years and years. And I do mean years. In 2010 some of these houses looked like the furniture had come straight out of a 1970's magazine! Whatever the house is furnished with is what you get. Just in case you are wondering, it is quite hard to decorate around old furniture, outdated appliances and ugly cabinets. Not to mention walls covered with hideous wallpaper. Ugh!

There are two ways the church can provide a house to the pastor and his family. The first one and unfortunately not common at this time, is through a housing allowance. This allows the pastor to purchase or rent a home to his own liking in an area that he is happy with. The second, and most often utilized, is the furnished parsonage.

The furnished parsonage (house) seemed like a good way to do things back in the 1960's and 1970's. But after several decades of providing furnishings for ministers in church owned parsonages, it became apparent that many ministers were nearing retirement age with no possessions and nowhere to live. They had been required to live in a church provided parsonage with church provided furniture and now they were going to retire without a home or furniture to put in it!

I am afraid. Yes, very afraid. This could be us fifteen years from now! We are middle aged, and we have nowhere to live when we retire. At least we have our own living room and bedroom furniture, so we will have somewhere to sit and sleep when retirement comes. **Note to Parents:** Raise your children well and always keep a healthy relationship. You never know when you are going to need them to take care of you!

Two Months to Pack: Now to the packing part. I do not think I am going to be very good at this. I am a procrastinator. A BIG one! My husband keeps telling me I need to call and set up appointments for movers to come and give us quotes. I put it off for at least three weeks. Then, sometime in April I got on the internet and Goggled "Local Movers". I found several sites and started making some calls. I got a lot of recordings. Then I tried filling out information on company web pages. That was hard because they wanted to know specifically what we were moving. There was a list of items to check off. But they did not have a "hot tub", "elliptical machine" "stationary bike" or "treadmill" on their lists. Nor did they have a giant fireplace mirror, bicycles or any of the crap in our garage. I am not sure how all this works. How can an on-line quote be accurate? It wants to know how many boxes I will have. What?! How the heck do I know? I have to schedule this move a month ahead of time and I cannot pack our stuff that early. I finally found a company that would come out and look at our things and then give me a quote. They quoted the move and they quoted what it would cost to pack it all up. I was excited. We originally thought we would get two or three quotes, but this one came in under budget, so we took it. My husband told me to e-mail the quote to the new church. I did and then I breathed a sigh of relief. I would not have to stress about packing all this stuff up. I quickly shoved this move to the back of my mind and began planning a 70's themed going away bash as our last party at our current parsonage.

One evening, while we were sitting around talking to friends, the subject of packing came up. I remarked that we would have the movers do it because the entire quote came in under budget. My husband quickly corrected me, saying that packing was not an allowed expense.

Now I am totally confused and annoyed and extremely stressed. I cannot pack all this stuff! I thought I did not have to worry about it. OMGosh! So, the fight/argument began. We finally had to call a truce over the miscommunication concerning the movers packing us up and I accepted the fact that I was going to be doing it. I began packing a couple of boxes a night.

One week and twenty or so boxes later, I sent an e-mail to the new church, explaining that we understood that the church was not responsible for packing expenses and that although it had been part of the quote, we did not expect them to pay for those expenses. I would be happy to get a quote with the packing part removed, if need be.

Later that evening, during dinner at a local restaurant, I received a telephone call from a truly kind gentleman from the new church, advising me that it would be okay to have the movers help us with some of the packing. I graciously thanked him and then hung up. I am now a much less stressed person. I have decided to continue to pack boxes every night and will hopefully finish by the time our move date arrives. However, now I know that if I do not finish, I have a backup plan. Whew!

Three Weeks Prior to the Move: Sorting and tossing and packing. It is hot, I am sweating (possibly menopause) and not in the best of moods, but I can and will do this. I must protect my husband who, *fortunately for him*, has a moving phobia. (No really, he does)! Besides that, the truth is I would rather him not be here while I am trying to pack, although I do refuse to pack up the garage stuff.

I forgot to mention that we have two grown children living with us that are going to be moving elsewhere when we move to the new parsonage. The problem is, they do not know where they will be moving too. They just know that they do not want to come with us.

It is hard to take care of an eighteen-year-old that knows everything. Eighteen is NOT old enough to be on your own. However, due to some bad choices that he has made, he cannot live with us unless he makes some radical changes in his lifestyle. With that in mind, I cannot kick him out, either. He is not old enough. What is a mom to do?! He says he does not want to live with us. He wants to get an apartment with his friends. At least he will not be alone, but I need to know that he is okay. After all, ...He is my baby.

Then there is the twenty-three-year-old. He has his life all together; except for one thing. His job is moving to Rhode Island and he is not. He does not like it there. So, he is on the hunt for a new job. He has saved up some money, but I do not want him to deplete his savings or his 401K. Again, what is a mom to do? He could come live with us, but he does not want to. He wants to be on his own. I understand that too, but ...He is my baby.

And last but not least, my twenty-five-year-old that lives five minutes away, is moving to Rhode Island, with his job, in less than a week. I am proud of him and happy for him. But I hate to see him go so far away, because ...He is my baby.

I am a wife and a mom. And I am not just any wife, I am a Pastor's wife, and I am Super mom. I feel the need to take care of everyone, even if the men in my house are driving me crazy.

I am really struggling with all the moving in my family. Empty Nest Syndrome has crept up quietly and is about to punch me in the gut and leave me drowning in my tears. My husband, on the other hand, has longed for a time when it could be "just the two of us". He loves all the boys, but rightfully says it has never been "just the two of us" ever since we got married. I hope he can handle me crying, at least for a while.

The packing continues, for soon we will move into a very large, very empty, very big, very quiet, very lonely four-bedroom house. I guess this time must come for all moms. I hope I can handle it with dignity. I must focus on the positive things. As I told my husband, now we will be able to sit at the kitchen table in our underwear if we want to. We can sleep with the bedroom door open and even wander around nude if we so desire. We promise to keep the curtains closed. Haha!

We will be able to watch the big TV whenever we want, and the house will even be clean most of the time. I should be happy. I know in time, that I, like all moms, will accept my empty nest until I can fill it with the laughter, sticky fingers and hugs and kisses of grandchildren.

Okay, I got a little sidetracked. Let us get back to the move. How MANY rolls of tape could it possibly take? Maybe I am using too much. I have packed boxes and taped them up and now I cannot move them! I am a weakling. I have to leave them right where I pack them. That makes for a nice obstacle course throughout the house! Eventually, someone (of the male persuasion) will move them to the top of a stack, for me.

So, guess what room I packed first? The room that would make the least sense, of course. I told you I was not going to be very good at this. So, I started with the kitchen! I packed the dishes, glasses, pots and pans, small appliances and plastic containers. Yes, I still have a month to go. At least I did not pack the coffee pot and we always have the grill to cook on. It was just so easy to sit in the kitchen floor and pack and sort. I figured we could eat on paper and plastic plates for a while.

After the kitchen, I moved on to packing up knick knacks. I know it is another strange choice. I am packing up all the stuff that makes a home feel like a home. What was I thinking? Anyway, I have not quite finished with all that yet but there is no turning back now. I might as well finish. At least now I am thinking about what to do next. I am trying to be a bit more reasonable with my choices. Maybe I will work on the hall closet next.

It is almost like I have never moved before. I cannot remember the previous times. I cannot remember how or when I packed boxes. I do not remember the moving days. I do not remember unpacking. I have moved seven times (in the same city). I am starting to scare myself. Could I have blocked all these instances out of my mind? Or am I losing my mind? I know stress can play terrible tricks on your mind, body and spirit! What I do remember is that my previous moving circumstances occurred during incredibly stressful times in my life. Maybe that is why I cannot quite remember. Hmmm, I do not like this subject anymore.

I can say that I am excited about this move. I am looking forward to our new home and I like the town that we are moving too. I am sad about moving away from family and friends, but it is not that far. I must focus!

Two Weeks and Counting: I HATE moving! I hate everything about it. Darn these boxes. I cannot find the tape,

AGAIN! I cannot find a permanent marker. I have bought at least six of them! I hate this whole process. Yes, "hate" is a strong word. I have packed thousands of boxes...okay, forty or so. And it does not look like I have done a thing.

What is worse is that my husband keeps saying things like:

"You should be about done with that room shouldn't you?"

"There isn't really that much more to do."

"It shouldn't take very long to finish up."

While I have been muttering things under my breath, like:

"I'm going to hurt him." OR

"Why is he laying on the bed while I pack?" AND

"If he asks me ONE more time what I'm doing...!"

And tell me this, WHY does the church committee need to come in and paint before I move out? Where am I supposed to put our STUFF? Do they think I LIKE the smell of paint, or that I like feeling like I need to play hostess to people in my house when every glass, plate and utensil is packed in a box somewhere? I know it must be done. It is not their fault that it all has to happen so quickly. I am sure I will be better at this the next time around.

Our official move day is June 29th. Our new parsonage is not going to be ready to move into until June 30th. This could have been a real problem, but because my parents live nearby, we can stay with them, while we are homeless. That is the okay part. The kicker is that our stuff is being loaded onto the moving truck on the 27th (we mistakenly thought we could move in the new parsonage early). We have a three-day window of nothingness! I guess I will just wander.

Anyway, back to the packing nightmare. It has been an absolute mess. Every day is punctuated with tears. I prefer going to work as opposed to being at home. We have two children moving in different directions with their stuff going with them. We are trying not to mix our stacked boxes with their stacked boxes. That is of course when I can even get them to PACK a box. Have you ever tried to motivate an 18-year-old and a 23-year-old? I think we are all praying for the "packing fairy" to come and save us from this real-life drama.

Now I am thinking back to when I said I was looking forward to this move. Silly me, I should have known better, but I am an optimist. I always expect things to go smoothly. I prefer to live life in a state of perpetual niceness, happiness and beautiful colors (no I am not on drugs). I do sometimes get disappointed, but I like to expect and look forward to the best possible scenarios. However, in this case, it just did not happen. I have decided that when we have to do this again, and we will, that I will take a month off work. Maybe go on an extended vacation and then come home when it is all over. Or, perhaps, I will pay the estimated $2,000 and have packers come in, pack everything in a day and be done with it. I have decided that no matter how much it costs, it is worth it. The daily arguing and the resulting tears are not! But what is done is done. To quote my sweetheart of a brother-in-law..."it is what it is" and we WILL survive this! After all, God will not give us more than we can handle, right? My husband is close to melt-down mode, but we have some wonderful friends that are keeping him focused and helping him work through it all. Also, his brother David, was a God send! Understanding that Jeff had a phobia about packing and moving, he graciously, in one weekend drove all the way from Nashville Tennessee, packed up our entire garage, pulled Jeff out of his gloom and drove back home.

Oh yeah, remember that closet that I was going to pack "next". It still is not done. It is the last big thing we have left to do. The rest is down to scattered stuff here and there.

One week until moving day: It is also Father's Day and my birthday. A Big one. Guess what my loving husband did? He invited people over to celebrate. A cookout and cake and ice cream. I found out the day before said event.

"I invited some friends over for cake and ice cream, after church tomorrow," he says.

"What?" I reply.

"Just a few, it will be fun. It's your birthday and we should celebrate!"

"Ok", I said, "but just three couples. I do not want anything big. There is too much going on."

"Okay," he replied.

The NEXT DAY at church, I hear him asking people to come over for a cookout.

"Are you insane?" I ask. "We can't have a cookout! Everything is packed!"

"We still have the grill hooked up," he says, "everything will be fine."

"I suppose it will be, if you plan on flipping meat over on the grill with your fingers? What were you thinking!?" I ask in an exasperated tizzy.

"Don't worry, it will be okay," he says.

To get the full impact of this planned party, you must know that my husbands' idea of a cookout is not the same as what everyone else's idea of a cookout is. To most people, a cookout is burgers and dogs, potato salad, baked beans, pasta salad, watermelon and deserts. To my husband, a cookout is him preparing meat. That is all, nothing else. Sometimes I think that he thinks the rest of the food at a cookout just magically appears.

"I asked people to bring a side dish," he says.

"People? How many people?" I ask accusingly. "This is supposed to be just a few of our closest friends. I am not up to a party. My back hurts and I am tired. The packing has really worn me out!"

"Don't worry about anything," he says. "Just send an e-mail or text message and tell people to bring their own plates and utensils."

This is when I find out how many people are coming...or so I thought. I sent out eight messages. I was not really happy. Mostly I was just overwhelmed. I lay down on the bed to rest for a few minutes before the arrival of our guest. My husband was already lying down, tired as usual, after preaching two sermons and Sunday school.

Then the fight began...

"Did you pick up a cake?" He asks.

"Nooooo!" I reply with an attitude.

"Are you going to?" He asks.

"NO, I'm NOT!!! Why would I pick up a cake for my OWN birthday?" I snapped.

Please know that I love ALL our friends. But I was tired and had an atrocious headache. Do you know how hard it is to smile and be happy when you have a headache?! Of course you do!

So, he left in a huff to get the cake. Soon afterward, eighteen people arrived to celebrate. YES, eighteen! I did not speak to my husband for the rest of the night. However, everybody did bring their own eating utensils and plates, and someone even brought grilling utensils. All in all, it did turn out to be a nice evening... minus the headache.

16

TRANSITIONING

One week later I was living in my own personal nightmare! Every day was punctuated by tears. We were fighting constantly, and the tension was horrific. I was being pulled in too many directions and I was trying to keep everybody happy. It was impossible. Trying to find clothes to wear to work every morning was a chore. We had not eaten at home in a month (remember, I packed the kitchen first). I had packed a suitcase and taken a carload of stuff over to my mom and dad's, including refrigerator and freezer contents. I unload the refrigerator/freezer stuff into their refrigerator / freezer, but the rest of the stuff remained in my car. I am convinced that when you load stuff into a car, it expands. I could not see out of the side window or the back window. There was no room for passengers. My car, complete with pillows and blankets, looked like a homeless person lived in it. Wait! We ARE homeless!

Anyway, now that our personal things are at mom and dads and we, the boys, the dog and the guinea pig are at mom and dads and the boxes are taped up and ready to load, I think I am finally ready. Bring on the movers!!!

MOVING DAY

They movers arrived at 9:30 a.m. and had us completely loaded up by 2:30 p.m.. Upon their departure, we began the final stages of cleaning. Left to finish up was the refrigerator, the kitchen sinks and counters and vacuuming the floors. My husband believes that you should always leave a place better than you found it. Our current parsonage committee had arranged to replace screens and paint. Jeff had replaced all the blinds, shampooed the carpets and cleaned the bathrooms. I am sure I must have sweated off 10 pounds in the last few days. Those scales packed away in a box somewhere better have some good news for me the next time we meet!

We turned in our keys and for two days we were officially homeless, without an address or a place to call our own. Three days later the new church had completed repairs to the parsonage. It had undergone a home makeover and was looking beautiful. We would be able to off load our things from the moving truck and begin the next chapter in our lives. We were excited.

The moving company dispatcher called me at work and said the moving truck would be at the parsonage between 9:00 am and 11:00 am. I immediately called my husband, who was anxiously waiting at our new home. Then, as had become typical with our lives lately, there was a snag! When they got to within a tenth of a mile from our house, everything came to a screeching halt. It just so happens that a beautification project was in process on this street and as a result the road was a bit torn up in preparation for moving overhead lines and wires to underground cables. The moving truck was unable to get through all the construction. Telephone calls were made and in a short time the moving truck, filled with our earthly lives, made a grand entrance into our new little town. Half a dozen men, dressed in bright orange vests, stopped working and stopped traffic in both directions to allow for its passage. When they did get to our house, the men from the moving company were even more annoyed that they could not park on the street where they would have easy access to the back of the truck and be better able to maneuver the boxes and furniture. To make matters worse, the driveway was on a slight incline thus making it rather difficult to back out of and onto the street, which had been narrowed due to the construction. I sure was glad that my husband was taking care of this end of the move!

We had carefully labeled our boxes in hopes that they would be put in the rooms that the labels indicated, thus lessening our need for physical labor. Well, maybe not so carefully and maybe not *all* of them, but most of them. We thankfully and gratefully estimated that about eighty percent of the boxes actually made it to the designated locations. While sweating and grumbling, the movers emptied the truck of all our belongings in approximately five hours. We were happy. They were not! Their goal was to get paid and get the heck out of Dodge!

As a result of our labeling finesse, we had boxes piled in every room and although this was better than trying to move them or carry them ourselves, it was a frightful thing to see. Who knew it could take three big boxes just to pack up bathroom stuff from ONE bathroom? And that is not even including towels. How on Earth had we accumulated so much stuff? Why do we have so many bottles of shampoo and where did all this toothpaste come from?!

On to phase two of this move. Let the unpacking begin!

HOME SWEET HOME

Thank God for the compassionate and caring church family that we had not even met yet and for old friends with an enormous amount of energy. Our new church family had filled our refrigerator with dinners, sandwich meats and cheeses, chips, fruit, salad, soda and juice. A welcome basket filled with goodies had been placed on our kitchen table and there was even a monogrammed towel hanging on the oven door. The parsonage was beautifully painted and decorated with the parsonage furniture. Now all we had to do was incorporate our own furniture and begin unpacking boxes. Where to begin?

Jeff had gotten our bed re-assembled and made up during the day, so the first evening, after I got home from work, I kind of just wandered around in a daze and then we went to bed. The next morning, I got up bright and early and started in on the kitchen. The parsonage was scheduled to receive new appliances and I had to clear the area. Later that evening, my friend Kathy came over and started unpacking boxes in the Den. She was a Godsend, a whirlwind in a slow-moving household. Then, in a show of support for my husband in his new appointment, two of our special friends came to our new church on our first Sunday and then stayed all afternoon to continue the unpacking process. Empty boxes were flying out the door. Furniture was assembled and mirrors were attached to dressers. I do not know what we would have done without them. Actually, I do...I would STILL be unpacking boxes. When I get overwhelmed, I just kind of shut down. I am sure that if it were not for Kathy and Ben, that at this very moment my husband and I would still be living in cardboard box hell! Once she got those out-of-control boxes down to a manageable size, I could regain control of myself and them! I must say that our new home is VERY nice. Next is the yard...another ugh!

17

WEDDINGS

Some ministers like to perform weddings, some do not. Although my husband does a beautiful wedding ceremony, he prefers to do funerals. More about that later.

Jeff believes that most weddings are about the party. Typically, the bride and groom do not put much thought into the ceremony. What they care about is the wedding dress, and the flowers, the tuxedos and the bride's maid's dresses. They put a lot of thought into what kind of champagne to have and who they want to cater their reception. They are worried about the photographer and videographer and how good their pictures will turn out. They are busy planning their honeymoon. At some point the wedding ceases to be a religious ceremony. Maybe it never was.

Some are just fashion shows or flagrant displays of wealth.

WEDDING FLUFF

It is difficult to understand why people who do not attend a church, want to get married in one. Some have never or rarely even been inside of a church. Some have only been in a church to attend someone else's wedding or funeral. A few are Holiday pew sitters. They come for services at Christmas time, Thanksgiving or Easter and sit with other family members who have been tryng to get them to come to church. Nevertheless, whatever their beliefs are, when it is time to say, "I do", they start searching the internet for a church. Not just ANY church. They must do their research and find one with a center aisle. Most brides dream about walking down that aisle. They romanticize about it. They want a storybook wedding. Who can blame them? It's every little girls dream!

The nagging question for engaged couples is this: IS it important where you get married? I think that some people must believe that if they get married in a church, God will bless their marriage. Why else would non-church goers want to get married in a church?

SO, will it be in a small church with just your family members and a few close friends? Will it be in a large church with a center aisle, lots of flowers and everyone you know? Will the ceremony be performed by a "Justice of the Peace", or will you have a minister? Maybe you will get married on a beach, on a ship, in a backyard or in a living room. Perhaps it will be in a ballroom at a five-star hotel. It could be in an ancient castle or a beautiful flower garden. The possibilities are endless. But that is not all... Will you have a limousine, a horse drawn carriage or your own vehicle? Maybe you will have alcohol to toast the marriage. Maybe you will not.

Unfortunately, couples often forget to invite God to share in this special day in their lives, the very day that they asked Him to bless them and their marriage vows. There are so many other details to take care of that God gets pushed to the side. They do not think about God again...until they call the minister for marriage counseling.

Undoubtedly, it is a tough concept for the newlyweds of today, many of whom come from broken homes and single parent households. Of course, there are certainly people who take their wedding vows and the ceremony very seriously. They understand the lifelong commitment.

When asked to perform a wedding ceremony, my husband first speaks with the couple and explains the procedures that must be followed for the ceremony to take place. Most couples are surprised thinking all they have to do is show up and say, "I do", while a few welcome the requirements with open hearts and minds.

One of these requirements is that the couple be available for a six-week (once a week) one hour counseling session. During this session, they discuss their ideas of what their marriage expectations are.

The couple, separately, completes an online Compatibility Inventory called "Prepare & Enrich". The responses are then reviewed by Jeff and the couple. There are no wrong or right answers. Its purpose is to show a couple where their relational strengths and weaknesses may be.

On a side note, this Compatibility Inventory is also particularly good for married couples to reevaluate and improve on their relationship. Circumstances and everyday life choices over the years will change our individual perception on our martial relationship. This inventory is a good tool for determining areas where a little work may be helpful.

Weddings, just like people come in all sizes. The ceremony may be small and intimate or the blowout of the year. Whatever the setting, most couples like to have a rehearsal. It seems to calm the wedding day nerves ever so slightly. Jeff feels that the wedding rehearsals is one of his most annoying tasks and by far, the most difficult to orchestrate. The Bride, the Groom, the mother and The Mistress of Ceremonies are rarely in agreement about how the ceremony will take place. The rehearsal can become tense and often time tears become an unwelcome hindrance. It becomes blatantly clear that someone must take control. So, when the participants are clearly at an impasse the minister steps in and takes over. The minister knows what must be done and if he does not want to spend the next three or four hours trying to run through a rehearsal that should only take thirty minutes, he has to risk a few hurt feelings. My husband usually starts his rehearsals by asking the bride what she has in mind and then he assumes command. Keep in mind that at this point, everyone is not happy which means that somehow, he has failed. Of course, this is only his perception. He has performed over 300 weddings and is quite good at it.

I often attend weddings that my husband officiates. He likes for me to go with him and I like to be there to support him. It calms his nerves to see me sitting out in the audience or just to know that I am there. And it means that he will have someone to sit with at the reception. I usually hold the marriage license for him and help him get his robe on when it is time. I enjoy his ceremony, as it contains a little bit of history about marriage and symbols. I also enjoy seeing the brides in their dresses. All brides are absolutely stunning in their wedding dresses whether they be white or ivory, short or long, full or form fitting, intricately laced or plain. I have yet to see a bride that was not beautiful. Women, young and old, have a beautiful aura around them on their wedding day.

I am also intrigued by what other people wear to weddings. I would never go to such a special occasion without dressing up in my Sunday best. However, it has become apparent to me that the "Sunday best" wear is slowly disappearing. I have seen older women attend formal weddings wearing slacks and a blouse. Younger women and teenagers wear party dresses and young men wear shorts and flip flops! People watching is at its best during a wedding reception.

Receptions are the main reason I go to weddings with my hubby. It is not what you are thinking, but yes, I do like the free food! There are usually assigned tables and if I am not there my husband sits with six or seven people that he does not know and who are uncomfortable because they had to sit with the preacher guy. At least if I am with him, everyone is a little more comfortable. If we have a glass of wine or a beer (Yes, we are Christians) our table guests will look at us like we are real people! I must mention that like a police officer, my husband does not drink until he is "off duty", which is after the blessing has been said. So, while I sit at this table with a bunch of strangers that may or may not talk to us, I watch the bride and groom and how they interact with each other and their guest. I determine by their actions whether I like them as a couple and if I think they will make it or not. I know that seems a little judgmental, but really its not. Just a game I play to entertain myself amongst people I do not know. If I did not mention it before, I am basically an introvert, so my whole existence with Jeff, outside of family time, is out of my comfort zone. Fortunately, I have become quite adept at hiding my uncomfortableness, thus you will see me talking and laughing with strangers, like it is the most natural thing in the world.

Again, I digress! Back to whether a couple will survive their marriage vows....

If the groom is hanging out with his family and friends and the bride is hanging out with hers, then I label them as "not going to last" couple. If they are visiting with their guest together as Husband and Wife, they pass my first test. I watch them throughout the reception or at least until we can gracefully bow out. I watch the first dance and if we stay long enough the cake cutting. I do not go for cramming the cake into each other's face. I think it shows a lack of respect. This is when I make my final determination. I know it seems like a harsh little game to play and I do not share it with anyone except my husband. It is just that so many young people get married without a clue as to what marriage is about.

Footnote: My pet peeve about wedding receptions is that they always wait until the end to cut the wedding cake. Half of the guests have already left. We almost always miss the cake. I want cake!!! I say introduce the wedding party and cut the cake! Eat dessert first!! Some people (mainly the minister) have to work in the morning! We cannot stay out late partying with people we do not even know that will most definitely have more fun when we leave.

Weddings can be unpredictable and there is always the possibility of surprises, mayhem and disorder!

It should also be noted that the officiating minister often will not get paid. People seem to think that spending two to four hours with the wedding rehearsal on Friday night and two to four hours for the wedding on Saturday is "just part of his job". Apparently, so are the hours spent in premarital counseling. Jeff never sets a fee or asks for money. He is afraid that it will put a bad taste in people's mouths, regarding the church. People do not think about the time these events take away from the minister's personal lives.

18

A DIVORCED CHRISTIAN. HOW COULD THAT BE?!

I knew of one woman who had been married three times. The first two times were in the church she had attended her whole life. She loved her church and that was where she wanted to be. Although neither marriage lasted, it was not for lack of trying. She thought she was doing everything right, but soon realized she had made bad choices regarding her selection of men. Still, she tried to keep her promises and adhere to her marital vows. She prayed, and cried and begged, but it was not to be. She felt like a failure. "What Christian," she said to herself, "Gets married and divorced, not only once but TWICE!?" That was not the way it was supposed to be. She fought to pull herself out of a lingering sadness and regain her self-esteem.

The days trudged on and before too long, she fell head over heels in love with another man. He was all she had dreamt of she knew this one was right. This relationship felt completely different. This man was a Christian. He loved God and he loved her. They planned their wedding and their honeymoon. They planned and they planned. Well, nothing went as planned. Their destination wedding location did not work out. The paperwork was completed at the last minute and horrors upon horrors...she could see her panty lines through her dress! However, they would not be deterred. They knew this relationship was right and so they regrouped. They pulled everyone together, including the minister, and found an available location. They ended up getting married in an Irish Piano Bar. The ceremony was just as spiritual and as special as it would have been in a church. They were just as happy. What the woman had learned was that it really did NOT matter WHERE you got married. What mattered was that you remembered to invite God to the wedding, no matter where it took place and that you invited him to be part of your marriage.

I KNOW THIS WOMAN VERY WELL ?

19

An Unwanted Bride

There was one wedding rehearsal that made my husband particularly uneasy about the wedding that was to take place the following day. As I often did, I attended the rehearsal with him. If it is in a church, I usually meet the couple and some of the family and then sit in a pew near the back and away from all the activity. I do not intrude on the wedding festivities or my husband's duties. I am there for moral support and to help my husband if he needs anything. Otherwise, I just sit and enjoy. I never tire of hearing his wedding ceremony.

This rehearsal was set for the evening before the wedding. The couple was asked to stress to the participants how important it was that everybody be there on time. The bride and groom arrived ten minutes early, as did most of the family. Some trickled in a few minutes late. There seemed to be a lot of tension in the air. Perhaps just a nervous bride I thought. But as I sat and listened, it became apparent that the bride's family did not particularly care for the groom. The couple stood off to the side not really mingling with the family and the bride seemed to be close to tears. I felt bad for the young couple. They were probably in their mid-twenties and were taking care of all the wedding arrangements, themselves. I had a lot of time to observe the family dynamics because the father of the bride and one of her sisters, a bridesmaid, had not arrived yet. The father came in about thirty minutes late. The sister was almost an hour late! She was not in any hurry and was in no way apologetic for her lateness. Nor did she offer an excuse. The bride and her sister exchanged some harsh words and my husband hurriedly moved to begin the rehearsal before things got out of hand. The bride's maids (sisters) walked down the aisle giggling and making faces. They giggled all through the practice. They told the bride that when the minister asked if anyone objected to the marriage that they were going to object! The bride had already succumbed to tears. They walked through the rehearsal once and my husband wrapped it up.

The next day we arrived at the church twenty minutes prior to the wedding. Everyone arrived on time and things seemed better. The bride was beautiful, and she was ready to get married. The ceremony began. The bridesmaids walked down the aisle with smiles on their faces and they were not giggling. So far, so good! They came to the part where the minister asks if anyone can show just cause why this couple should not legally be married. No one uttered a word. I breathed a sigh of relief. The minister then asked, "Who gives this woman to this man to be lawfully married in holy matrimony?" The father loudly proclaimed "Her mother and I do. GLADLY". A soft but audible gasp was heard from the wedding guests. I was appalled. This most special day of this woman's life and her parents could not wait to get rid of her. I hoped with all my heart she was marrying this man because she loved him and not because she wanted to get away from the digs and jabs of her uncaring and cold family, though I could understand if she was! I felt so bad for her and was just praying that she would not let them ruin her day. I do not even remember the reception. Perhaps they did not have one. If they did, we probably did not go. My husband does not like to be in stressful family situations.

20

THE HILLBILLY WEDDING

What is a hillbilly? I know that some people use the term in a derogatory way and I certainly do not want to offend anyone so, like all computer savvy people of this decade, I Googled it. Several internet dictionaries describe a hillbilly as "a person from a backwoods area". Now, of course, not knowing exactly what "backwoods" meant, I had to Google that as well. I learned that backwoods means any remote or secluded area. As you will see, this is exactly the type of location where Jeff had been asked to officiate a wedding ceremony.

He had met with a young couple several times to discuss their wedding plans, including the date, location and time that the ceremony would take place. On the morning of the wedding, he gathered his robe and ceremony book and headed out the door. It was a beautiful warm summer day, perfect for an outdoor country wedding.

He started out an hour early, figuring a forty-five-minute drive. He typically arrives fifteen minutes prior to the start of the service. There were a lot of long winding roads, up and over hills, around curves and past little mom and pop stores. Since all of the meetings with the couple were in his office, he had not actually been to the wedding location. He did have handwritten directions but was starting to get a little nervous. The directions were not great, and he was not familiar with the area. It was almost time for him to be there and he had begun to drive up and down the same roads looking for the right place.

If you have ever driven much in the country, than you know that country roads are notorious for not having signs. People that live in the country learn how to follow directions by landmarks. They recognize and know fields, trees, houses, corners and corrals by name. Country people have an entirely different sense of direction. They sense and notice things that we, as city people, do not even see. You may hear someone say "Turn left at the pecan tree on Jones corner and keep going past Mr. Hyman's field. Then you will see a big red barn on the right. Just a piece up from that turn left and you will see Mr. Joe's store."

The roads seemed to curve and wind, going on forever. The directions were not great, and he was not familiar with the area. It was almost time for him to be there. He was starting to sweat. Thinking that he must be in the right area, he had begun to drive up and down the same roads looking for the right place.

This particular incident takes place in the 1980's so, cell phones are a thing of the future. Eventually he came across a pay phone. He frantically called the number he had, which belonged to the bride. No answer! He dialed the groom's number. No answer! Everyone within a 20-mile radius was most likely at the wedding.

He finally found the right place by driving around until he came upon a house with a massive number of cars parked in the yard. He was one hour late! Although it is true that the wedding cannot start without the minister, the reception most certainly can.

The restless crowd grew tired of waiting and the bride and groom decided to start the reception. They were none too happy when Jeff arrived. By now, most of the guest were well on their way to being drunk. Jeff made his apologies and immediately proceeded to try and get the ceremony started. He managed to holler, loud enough to be heard over the partying, that they were going to begin the service. Still drinking and smoking the guest stumbled over to the event seating. They finally quieted down as the bride and groom took their places. Jeff had the couple facing him ready to begin. Comically, he had to ask them to put down their beer and cigarettes so they could face each other and hold hands as they said their vows. As soon as he pronounced them husband and wife, someone shouted "DOVES". Immediately people bolted from their chairs, ran for their vehicles and quickly returned wielding shot guns.

Much shouting and shooting commenced and Jeff quickly fled for his life, leaving a trail of dust behind, unnoticed by the gun toting hillbillies.

Kind of gives "shotgun wedding" a whole different concept, doesn't it?

21

JULY 4TH WEDDING

Holiday weddings seem like a bad idea to me, but I can understand the reasoning. The out-of-town guest will have an extra day for travel, extra time to spend with other family members gathered for the wedding and need to take less time off from work. Unfortunately, I think that is where the reasoning stops. The bride and groom forget that the traffic will be much more congested, the hotels will be more expensive, restaurants will be more crowded and there will usually be some type of public festivities, depending on the holiday. Having a wedding on a holiday weekend can teeter on the edge of disaster depending on the location where the ceremony is to take place.

My husband had one such wedding that was to take place in a park area next to the beach. The older couple, in their mid-forties, wanted to have a simple wedding with the beach and the bay as a backdrop. They had spent much time together at this beach and it held fond memories for both of them. Also, the two of them had lived in the area most of their lives and this beach held some fond childhood memories for them as well.

The place they chose was a medium sized concrete circle with cement benches and a 10' replica lighthouse encircled with a manmade moat. On the day of the wedding, family and friends arrived early to set up approximately 100 chairs. They were set up in two sections of nice even rows with a center aisle between them, that the bride would walk down. Flowers were placed in various locations, bows were tied to some of the chairs, an arbor was set up, speakers were placed, and a musician was ready and waiting. It was a beautiful sunny day, though very windy. The women who were standing around waiting for the ceremony to start where having to hold down their dresses with one hand and try to keep their hair out of their faces with the other. The whole setting was about two hundred yards from the road. The groom was in place. The bride arrived by limousine. It would have been a perfect setting IF it had been taking place in October or November.

Unfortunately, it was July 4th weekend. There were people everywhere. Music was blaring from boom boxes which were surround by families or friends having picnics or reclining on blankets and chairs. It was LOUD. Not just loud but mind numbing as music from different stations came from all directions. Of course, when the bride stepped from the limo, people's attention turned to her. No one bothered to turn their music down though, they only watched for a few minutes and then went back to their loud conversations.

People were milling all around the wedding area. Some walking, some were on rollerblades, some on skateboards and some on bicycles. At one point, two young boys rode up to the edge of the ceremony on their bicycles and dared each other to ride through the middle of the wedding. Luckily that didn't happen.

The wind was blowing so hard that the flowers were blowing over and bows were blowing off of the chairs. Hearing the minister or the bride and groom's vows, over the music and the wind, was all but impossible.

The wedding was performed, and the bride and groom seemed none the worse for wear. I think it may have been more nerve wracking for me than it was for them. It is difficult for the minister to concentrate on the wedding when there are so many distractions. I cannot imagine that it can be any easier for the couple.

22

HARLEY DUDE

One of the more uncomfortable weddings that Jeff offici-
ated was for an older couple who were part of a motorcycle
club. (When I refer to a couple as "older", I mean that the couple is over thirty years old). The ceremony was to be performed
on the balcony of their house, with their friends and family
watching from the front yard.

My husband ALWAYS wears a robe when he performs a
ceremony of any sort. However, this couple was adamant that
this was a very casual occasion and that everybody should be
wearing jeans or shorts and a t-shirt. They even went so far as
to give my husband a "Harley" T-shirt that they wanted him
to wear. He was uncomfortable with the whole casual deal and
told them that he really would like to wear his robe. But again,
they assured him that everyone would be wearing jeans and T-
Shirts.

We arrived at the home approximately twenty minutes early
and sure enough everyone was wearing jeans and T-shirts or

were in some type of "Harley" wear. My husband exhaled a sigh of relief. He met briefly with the bride and then the groom, found out where they wanted him to stand and then waited for the designated time.

When it was time to begin, the bridesmaids and best-man took their places. They were both dressed in formal wear. The bride and groom walked out wearing a white wedding gown and a tuxedo. My husband was taken aback and embarrassed that he was not robed. He made a joke about being under-dressed and proceeded with the ceremony.

I am not really sure why they didn't want him to wear a robe or why they wanted him in a Harley T-shirt. People do not understand the significance of the robe, so it does not make a difference to them. He was reluctant to go along with their request to begin with but ultimately, in an effort to please them, succumbed to their wishes. What I do know is that not wear-ing a robe will not happen again.

23

THE WEDDING THAT WASN'T

There are a few things that ministers learn after preparing for a wedding that goes awry. It is required, by law, that the bride and groom must obtain a marriage license prior to the commencement of the ceremony. My husband, who has to sign the license, is usually handed the license on the day of the wedding. He never had any issues arise, so never really gave the practice of requiring the license on the wedding day, a second thought. Until one day, fifteen minutes before a wedding ceremony was to take place.

Jeff went to the groom and asked, "Do you have the license?"

"I forgot to bring it" he replied.

"I can't perform the wedding without it. You will have to go and get it. We'll begin the service as soon as you get back."

The groom hedged a little and then admitted that he had not obtained one.

"I cannot perform the wedding ceremony."

"I promise I will get it first thing Monday morning. Everybody is here and the reception is already paid for and family has come from out of town. I promise I will get it on Monday," pleaded the groom.

"I'm sorry, it just isn't possible. It is against the law. I will talk to the bride and her parents and then make an announcement to the guests."

The bride, of course, was devastated and the parents were quite unhappy. However, what soon came to light was that the groom had deceived the bride. He had been married twice before and one of the divorces was not final. The bride had not been aware of her fiancé's previous marriages. My husband lost track of the couple, who ultimately blamed him for ruining their wedding day, because he would not marry them. He did learn that a year later they still had not married.

As a result of all this, he now asks for the marriage license the day before at the rehearsal. No license, No rehearsal.

FUNERALS

Jeff is of the opinion that people are more apt to gain spiritual knowledge and healing from words said at a funeral. People attending funerals do so out of respect for the deceased or the deceased's family. Some are hurting and seeking spiritual healing. Most ministers relish this opportunity to share God's love.

Generally, people do not think of a funeral home as a business. In fact, just like all businesses, they are operating to make a profit. It is imperative to keep this in mind while making decisions about your final resting arrangements. The services they provide are regulated by law and unless someone finds the "Fountain of Youth", we will all need their services someday. Although it may seem a bit morbid, it might be wise to shop around (when everyone is healthy). Find a funeral home that you are comfortable with, one that seems compassionate and honest. If you do not do your homework ahead of time and find yourself having to make decisions in direct relation to the death of a loved one, I can only say...TAKE YOUR PASTOR WITH YOU!

Your pastor cares about you. Your pastor cares about your budget and your state of mind. Your pastor most likely knows the personality of the deceased. He/she can help you make decisions that could be difficult at this particular time.

My husband once had a parishioner who went to a funeral home, alone, following the death of her war veteran husband. He was to have visitation and a memorial service at the funeral home and then would be buried in Arlington National Cemetery. Jeff visited her the next day and she showed him the paperwork and subsequent bill that she had been given. Jeff noticed that the funeral home had sold her a liner for the grave. He asked her why they would do that when Arlington provides a liner at no charge? She told him that the salesperson had told her that but, had said that theirs was better; that the one at Arlington would leak. The one they sold her cost $700.00!! My husband gently explained to her that all of them leaked, and he asked her if it was okay if he took her bill back to the funeral home to have it removed. She gratefully consented.

Jeff arrived at the funeral home with the bill and politely asked the salesperson to remove the charge. She was very unhappy with him and initially refused. She was adamant that their liner was better. Jeff told her that she had taken advantage of a distraught widow and sold her something that was unnecessary and furthermore she knew that ALL liners eventually leaked! The salesperson said she would not remove the charge unless the customer said to. She proceeded to call the customer who asked her to remove it immediately.

Fortunately, this kind of thing does not happen all the time, but it does happen. My husband is not a fan of elaborate funerals. He explains that expensive caskets look the same as inexpensive caskets when they are covered with dirt. He can help someone get the best deal for their money. Even though it is a difficult time, we must remember that the person is gone. Their spirit has left this place and all that remains is an earthly shell. Funerals can cost thousands of dollars. As far as I am concerned, when my time comes, be done with me. Do everything as cheaply as you can. No need for bling. I want that while I am still around! Do not remember me in an expensive coffin! Remember me in spirit. Remember me skinny (even if I am not) and smiling. Remember me happy and silly. Forget all the bad stuff and hold me close in your heart.

FUNERAL FOLLY

Mr. Jones, who was in his seventies, had been terminally ill for quite some time. He and his lovely spouse of many years had discussed his funeral service and made most of the arrangements prior to his passing. Among their discussions had been the option of having an opened or closed casket during the visitation. While Mrs. Jones preferred that the casket be open, Mr. Jones was not fond of the idea of having people come by to stare at his dead body and thus decided on a closed casket. It was a decision that Mrs. Jones understood and respected.

The time came when Mr. Jones quietly left this earth and traveled to his final resting place. Mrs. Jones said her final goodbye, kissed her beloved and left him in the care of the funeral director. She sat with Jeff and together they reminisced and prayed.

A few days later, she arrived at the funeral home for the visitation and the ensuing funeral. The casket was closed just as her beloved had requested. She stood close by his flower draped coffin, hugging and crying with the many loved ones and friends who gathered to share stories and offer their condolences. The room was filled with beautiful floral arrangements and the aroma of fresh cut flowers hung in the air. The low din of conversations could be heard throughout the room.

Jeff and the funeral director quietly stood off to the sides, the funeral director near the door and Jeff near the widow, in case they were needed for anything. The mourners continued trickling in a few at a time. One of the late arriving aunts strode up to Jeff and demanded to know why the casket was closed? He quietly and politely explained to her that the deceased had asked that the casket be closed, and they were honoring his request.

She turned and huffed off toward the casket, saying "People have driven a long way to see him and they should be able to." With that, she threw open the casket!

Gasps were audibly heard, and the widow was near fainting. The funeral director stared across the room at Jeff with a look or horror on his face. Jeff reciprocated the look of horror with his own stunned expression.

When a visitation is to be a closed casket, the body is not prepared quite the same as it would be if it were to be an open casket. Sometimes there are tiny details that might not necessarily be taken care of.

The funeral director sprang into action and rushed across the room to the casket. He quickly arranged the body as best he could and then re-closed the casket.

It seems there are surprises even where the dead are concerned.

25

YOU'RE BURYING HIM
WHERE?

We all attend funerals at some time in our lives. They seem to go smoothly as far as the untrained eye can tell. But sometimes things do go wrong. The funeral director and minister will most likely be aware of any issues, but the rest of us will be oblivious.

Back to the story of the gentlemen who was being buried in Arlington National Cemetery. A short service honoring his life was held at his home church. He was a retired war veteran and was to be buried at the national cemetery. What most people do not know is that you need to have an appointment to have a burial there. Ceremonies are performed with full military honors. Soldiers are stationed at the cemeteries for this sole purpose and it is a job served with great honor. Due to the nature of the ceremony, only a handful can be honored each day. At that time, there was a three week wait.

When the appointed time came, my husband met the family at the burial plot. The ceremony had not started but all the chairs were set up, the tent was erected, and the casket was in place. The widow looked a little perplexed. After a few minutes, she came over to my husband and said "I think this is the wrong place. What should I do?"

My husband said, "Are you sure?"

"Yes. I do not recognize any of the headstones. There is supposed to be one for me here, too."

My husband approached the funeral director and voiced their concerns. Following a quick check of the records, they found that they were indeed at the wrong plot.

"You are correct, sir. Let us proceed as usual and after everyone has left, we will move him to the appropriate place."

The widow agreed and the ceremony went on as planned. No one was the wiser.

26

EVIL?

Casual conversations can sometimes come back to haunt us. Sometimes we know things that we do not want to know. Sometimes we are sure of things that cannot be proven. Does evil exist today? You bet it does. Evil is a scary thing. Even murderers may not be truly evil. Maybe they snapped and struck out of passion or anger. Maybe they have true feelings of regret. We see meanness in people every day. We see rudeness and a serious lack of home training all around of us.

However, I believe premeditated murder *is* evil. Real evil has no regret. It takes on a whole different persona. You can see the presence of evil in a person's eyes. You may not notice it at first. It may be lurking behind a smiling face. That is the scariest part of all. When you find out you say to yourself "Why didn't I see that? I knew something wasn't right with that person." I am not talking about psychosis or the plethora of other personality disorders. Disorders and illnesses are certainly not to be confused with being evil. Evil comes from the soul.

Hopefully, you have never come face to face with evil. If you ever do feel evil around you, run away! Handling it is best left to professionals, i.e., ministers, priests, etc. Satan is hard at work every day. Our only weapon against this evil is Jesus Christ, the armor of God and the power of prayer.

27

A GHASTLY graveside

One rainy day in spring, a funeral was planned for a man who came from a very poor family. Jeff did not know the family but was called by the funeral home and asked to conduct a graveside service. The gentleman was to be buried in the church cemetery right beside the little country church that his family had attended for generations. Unfortunately, when it was time for the service, it had begun to rain heavily. The forecast was calling for heavy rains throughout the next several days. The funeral director moved the family, the casket and the flowers into the tiny church.

Following the service, the funeral director informed the family that they would proceed with internment after the rain passed. It had been a long snowy winter and an unusually rainy spring. The ground was completely saturated, the family had declined purchasing a liner and the hole was beginning to fill with water. The family was not happy about waiting and was insistent that they proceed immediately. The funeral director tried to explain to them that it was not a good idea.

The casket they had purchased was the least expensive casket that money could buy. It was made of plywood and literally held together by staples and glue. They were not persuaded.

The funeral director, Jeff and the pall bearers proceeded to carry the casket to the graveside. Jeff said a prayer and the casket was lowered into the ground. It had barely settled on the bottom, in several feet of water, when it began to come apart. Before they could get the dirt (that had become mud) to fill in the hole, the corpse was exposed! Ghastly and shocking! Audible gasps and whimpers from family members were heard over the commotion to get the dirt in the hole. I'm sure this is not the ending the family wanted to remember.

Purchasing the least expensive casket money can buy is not a bad idea and for some religions it is a requirement. So, whether it is because you are required to do so, because you are thrifty or because you just cannot afford anything more expensive, it may be wise to heed the advice of the funeral director and the minister!

28

RANDOLPH

This is a story about a man named Randolph. Randolph was an elderly cantankerous old man in his late nineties. He had lived a long, interesting life. He had gone blind during World War 1, after consuming a large amount of grain alcohol. He was also hard of hearing. Randolph lived with his daughter, who had Parkinson's disease, and his son in-law.

The son in-law, John, was formerly in the Army with specialized training, during World War II. He went into Germany before the end of the war conducting covert operations and to extract scientist and other important people for the United States Government. In essence, he was a spy!

John had worked hard most of his life and was now retired. Though it was an emotional drain on him, he was both physically and financially able to take care of his spouse and his father in-law. The three of them shared an exceptionally large house located in a mountainous area of Virginia. The summer months were hot but tolerable. However, the winter months were often bitterly cold. It was not unusual for the ground to be covered in a snowy white blanket.

Jeff knew John and his wife because they often attend the church that he was currently serving. Occasionally, they would bring Randolph to church with them. The old man and Jeff formed a special friendship (remember, we are not supposed to do that) and often talked of Randolph's War days and his resultant disabilities.

Randolph's lifetime hobby had been automobiles. At this time in his life, he owned three automobiles. Yes, a blind man with three cars! He had a fear of being stranded somewhere without transportation. He would ask someone to take him somewhere, and they would most likely be driving one of his cars. He was able to keep up with his passion for automobiles, current events and magazine articles of all kinds through the magic of technology. He had a machine that could scan books and magazines and read them back to him.

One day, Randolph found out that Jeff was driving a little over 200 miles a day traveling to and from seminary. He also learned that he was driving an unreliable old car and that at least once he had broken down on the side of the road. Randolph called Jeff over to talk to him about his car and ended up giving him a car, right there, on the spot, no strings attached. That is right, just GAVE him a car!

A year or so later, on a warm spring afternoon, Jeff was attending an event when he happened to see John. They shook hands and exchanged niceties. Jeff then asked him how Randolph was doing.

John replied, "I think he's going to die this winter."
Jeff laughed. "Oh no, he'll probably live to be in his 100's! He seems quite spry for an elderly person."
"No," said John. "I think he is going to die."

Spring came and went. Summer came and went. Then winter set in. It was an especially harsh winter. There was a lot of snow and ice, more than usual this particular year. Maneuvering through the slick winding mountain roads could be quite hazardous even for emergency vehicles.

There was one storm in particular that winter that brought the town to a standstill. The storm came in fast and furious. The wind was blowing a gale and the snow was coming down so fast that the town was having white-out conditions. The snow laden tree branches were popping and snapping under the heaviness of the snow. Power lines were coming down along with the branches. What looked like a beautiful picture that you might see on a Christmas card soon began to feel like a cold, camping trip in sub zero temperatures. People were stuck in their homes with no electricity for days. Even emergency vehicles and power trucks could not get to people. So, they dressed in layers and layers of clothes and if they were fortunate enough to have a fireplace, they huddled around it day and night, for whatever warmth they could obtain. When the storm finally subsided, people had to dig their ways out of their front doors, out of their driveways and then hope for plowed roads.

Tucked away, far back in the mountains, sat the home of Randolph, his daughter and his son in-law. Though they did not have any electricity, they did have a fireplace. After the roads were cleared and the town was mobilized again, John called the police to tell them that Randolph had passed away during the storm. Apparently, he froze to death in his bed. John and his spouse were fine.

Could it be death by natural causes or negligence or MUR-DER?

29

WALT REDMOND, JR.

(Musician / Singer / Songwriter)

My brother owned a restaurant bar in the downtown area of Hampton, Virginia. On Friday and Saturday nights he would have live entertainment, consisting of mostly local area bands or individual musicians. Jeff and I would try to go downtown a couple of times a month to support him and his business. We usually went on Monday through Thursday, when it was less crowded. Besides that, having a Sunday morning job definitely cuts down on the Saturday nightlife scene. Also, in order to be prepared for his Sunday morning services, my husband needs his beauty sleep! Even so, armed with our earplugs, because according to the younger set, we are old, we did occasionally go out on Friday or Saturday night. When we did, we would get to enjoy some of the local talent, and we befriended some of the waitresses as well as some of the local police. We met a lot of fine people, hanging out in this little downtown bar, (Yes, we are still Christians) one of whom was Walt Redman, Jr.

Walt was an amazing guitarist and songwriter with a great voice and a wonderful personality. We found out that he had started playing guitar when he was thirteen years old. As an adult, he had played on the East Coast from South Carolina to Vermont. He had also spent a few years in Austin, Texas, playing in different bands and in shows in Texas and all over California. When asked if he had ever opened for a "national act", he responded "Over the last fifteen years I have opened for several national acts such as Fog Hat, Styx, Billy Squire, Paul Rodgers from Bad Company, Blue Oyster Cult and I have shared the stage with Lita Ford opening for Kiss. This past year I did a show with Edwin McCain in Nags Head".

Walt was an INCREDIBLY talented man!

ADDICTION & SOBRIETY 2005

We also learned that, unfortunately, he had two serious problems. He was an alcoholic and a heroin addict. When things did not work out for him on the road, he had come back home to the place where he knew he was loved.

In December of 2005, Walt entered his first rehabilitation facility. When we met him in December of 2006, he had been sober and drug free for a year. He was proud of his one-year chip, and he had every reason to be! He was feeling good, had gotten his life back together and was dating a beautiful woman.

The first time we met Walt we were sitting in the bar, relaxing, talking with my brother and having a drink. Walt was playing guitar with his dad. We were really fascinated by his musical talent and were awed by how good he was. At this point, we did not know his background. We did not know that he had been on stage with the rich and the famous! We were just excited by the fact that we could still talk to my brother while Walt was playing and not have to insert our earplugs!

After he completed his first set of the night, Walt came over with a big friendly smile on his face and shook Jeff's hand. "I think I know you from somewhere!" Walt said.

"You look familiar too." replied Jeff.

After a "twenty questions" session, they figured out how they knew each other. Walt had attended a baptism that Jeff had performed some months earlier.

Following the next set, Walt came over to talk some more. He appreciated the fact that Jeff would joke with him and have a beer with him. Walt was drinking O'Doul's (non-alcoholic). He thought Jeff was cool. We soon learned that Walt was engaged, but he had not set a wedding date yet because he did not have a church or know a minister to perform the ceremony.

He looked at my husband and said "Hey! Will you marry me?"

"Sorry, I Can't", Jeff responded. "I'm already married!" (One of Jeff's favorite jokes.)

Walt did not think he would be comfortable in a church because he did not have the right clothes and he had a lot of tattoos. People would not want him there. They would stare at him, wouldn't they?

Jeff and I continued to build a relationship with Walt, going to his gigs at my brother's bar as well as a few other places. Over the months, we became Walt groupies. At one of his gigs, he had finished his first set and just before he walked off stage, he said, "I'm so excited" and he pointed to the left, "over here I have my tattoo artist", then he pointed to the right "and over here I have my minister!" Everyone laughed and cheered. Walt took his break, worked the room and then came over and sat with us for a few minutes.

MAY 2007

In May of 2007, Jeff had the honor of performing the wedding ceremony of Walt and his lovely bride. They said their "I Do's" on a beautiful Saturday evening in Walt Sr.'s lavishly decorated backyard. They seemed so happy. Their eyes sparkled when they were together. But, as we all know, looks can be deceiving and the promise of marital bliss was not to be. They were two quite different people. He was a handsome rock-n-roll, life of the party, work when I have a gig kind of guy. She was a beautiful, self sufficient, hard working, take care of herself woman. They were oil and vinegar.

She worked a full-time job during the day, and he played gigs with his band or had gigs with his dad at night. His sets would run into the early hours of the morning. Their schedules were a constant challenge. She, having to get up early for work the next day, could not be at all of his gigs, and he soon fell into some of his old habits.

The heroin addiction continued to be a daily struggle. Heroin is an extremely hard thing to beat, but Walt fought it with all his might. He had promised his bride that he would stay clean. I believe he genuinely wanted to. He loved her. But he loved the heroin even more. Not because he wanted to. His mind and body betrayed him. An addiction like this cannot be understood unless you have lived through it yourself or been close to someone who has. Addiction is a horrific thing. Eventually, you will have to walk away from the abuser and their destructive behavior. But you know in your heart that you can never truly walk away. You will always cry for them, for yourself, for lost time and for what could have been. You will never stop praying for them.

Heroin can be snorted, smoked or injected. Walt's choice was the needle. When injected directly into the bloodstream, it causes an incredible surge of euphoria. As with most drugs, the more heroin that it is used, the less effective it becomes, thus requiring more frequent doses. Chronic use of the drug will lead to a physical dependency. If stopped abruptly, either cold turkey in an effort to quit, or because it is unavailable, the body will go into a state of withdrawal. Major withdrawal can be very painful, causing muscle and bone pain, insomnia, diarrhea, vomiting, cold flashes and erratic muscle movement. In severe cases it can even cause death. Most users who want to quit go through a drug rehabilitation program. These programs help the patients with the withdrawal symptoms as well as working with them mentally to overcome the cravings.

Walt's bride had not been exposed to the world of drug abuse prior to this. She thought that once he quit and went to rehabilitation, which he had done prior to their marriage, he would be okay. Sadly, drug addiction and rehab rarely work that way. If the addiction is to be beat, the user must endure a lifetime of support meetings and self checks. They must be always accountable for their whereabouts and for every penny that they spend.

It is my belief that addicts that do not give their life and their addiction to God will not make it on their own.

WALT GIVES HIS LIFE TO CHRIST - 2008

Eleven months into their marriage, Walt fell off the wagon. His spouse discovered that he was drinking alcohol again and using prescription pills (valium and Oxycontin). The craving overcame him, and he admitted to her that he had relapsed two weeks prior. She called Jeff and 3 days later, after intensive counseling, Walt decided to go back to rehab. Jeff found a place that would take him, in North Carolina. We picked him, his bag and his guitar up the morning of his check-in date and started out on the 4-hour drive. Walt was very anxious. He talked incessantly and told us how much he loved and appreciated us. He was going to make it work this time. It was clear that he was on something. His actions were erratic. He was jumpy and restless. He told us he was talking valium to calm his nerves. I was sitting in the back seat, mostly resting after a prior day of chemotherapy. I wanted to give Walt and Jeff every opportunity to talk. Jeff praised Walt's music and his talent. He talked to him about how he could use this wonderful gift to glorify God. He continued to tell him that God loved him no matter what happened. He explained to him how Jesus died for his sins and that no matter how horrible they were that he could be forgiven. Walt was quiet for a little bit and then he said, "I want that." So, right there, driving down the highway, Walt asked Jesus into his heart. We prayed and we thanked God for Walt and prayed for the strength to get through the difficult days that lay ahead.

By the time we got to the rehabilitation facility, Walt was really starting to feel the effects of withdrawal. He had been popping pills every hour. When we pulled up, he started to gather his things. He said to me, "I'm going to give you these pills because I can't check in with them." He gave me a handful of Valium. We stayed with him through the initial registration and then we hugged him goodbye. He stayed in rehab for 4 weeks.

In May of 2008, Walt returned home, sober again, and in June he and his spouse were baptized into the family of Christ.

Walt really wanted to make his marriage work and hoped that when he got out of rehab things would be better with his wife. First, he would have to rebuild the trust that he had previously destroyed. She had conditions that he would have to adhere to before she could completely trust him again. They were reasonable conditions, and she had every right to expect a normal life.

He had been playing in bands since he was a kid. He was as addicted to the lifestyle as he was to the drugs. Unfortunately, this kind of lifestyle is often associated with drug use. The euphemism, "Booze, Drugs & Rock & Roll", is a reality. For Walt to stay off the drugs, he had to stay away from the lifestyle.

But for Walt, music was his life. That was all he knew. He was once asked by an interviewer: **What is one thing people should know about you?** His response was *"I will be playing music somehow somewhere for the rest of my life. It doesn't matter if it is for three people or for 3,000 people -- it's what I do and I love it."*

In fact, Walt wrote a song that was very special to him. He shared it in church one Sunday. It was called "PRAYERS". You can find a video of his performance on YouTube by typing in Walt Redman Prayers.

Prayers
By Walt Redmond Jr.

I've walked through dark places
and seen empty faces
That just seem so hollow to me
but now and then I catch a glimpse of a rainbow
that slowly would take me away

Oh Lord my Father can you hear all of my prayers
cause I'm reaching my arms out to you
And I'll hit my knees praying for another salvation
as I make my way home to you

I've been selfish and shamed
but you washed that away

lord lift me from all of my sins
And I'll start a new life one that makes me feel right
and gives me the strength to move on

Oh Lord my Father can you hear all of my prayers
cause I'm reaching my arms out to you
And I'll hit my knees praying for another salvation
as I make my way home to you

When the night time falls down
and the scenes in my head
just don't seem to want to slow down
I hold my hands tight as I'm closing my eyes
and I feel your warm spirit around

Oh Lord my Father can you hear all of my prayers
cause I'm reaching my arms out to you
And I'll hit my knees praying for another salvation
as I make my way home to you

He tried to change his circle of friends. I can only say that these people he called his "friends" were not really his friends. Friends do not encourage friends to "do drugs". They support their sobriety and try to intervene when necessary.

Sadly, slowly, his marriage began to fall apart. Jeff tried to help them. He counseled them as a couple, and he counseled Walt. The drugs are a ferocious enemy. They will tear a marriage apart. They create an emotional roller coaster and financial and physical burdens that in most cases are beyond repair. The newlyweds separated in 2008, after only 15 months of marriage.

OUT OF CONTROL - 2008

Walt continued to struggle with his sobriety and in October of 2008, he plunged, full-fledged, back into the world of heroin and his addiction spiraled out of control. On Christmas night, Walt appeared on the doorstep of his estranged spouse, confessing the magnitude of his addiction and asking for help. The next day, Jeff was working with him to get him back into rehab, again. On December 29th, 2008, he went one last time.

After another four weeks, Walt was home again. In a noticeably short time, we suspected that he was sliding back into the drug scene as we began to see less and less of him. His spouse was in constant contact with us and was doing her best to pick up the pieces and get on with her life. We began to hear rumors that there was another lady friend in Walt's life. He had just about stopped coming to church. Jeff continued to call him. Finally, Walt told us about his new friend. We did not think she was a drug user, but she was turning a blind eye to his addiction. She was enabling him. She was filling the void that his wife had left when she had put her foot down and demanded he stay on the straight and narrow, which was exactly what he had needed. He was so conflicted and torn. He told his wife that he wanted to be with her, but his actions said otherwise. He struggled with his faith. How could God love him?

His life came to a sad end one sunny Tuesday afternoon. On April 7th, 2009,

He was found sitting in a dark room with the curtains drawn, in front of his computer with a needle hanging out of his arm. He had accidently over-dosed and was dead.

His wife was devastated. Jeff was devastated. We were all devasted. We had failed. We had all tried so hard to help him. What more could we have done?

Walt left behind, a spouse, three beautiful children from previous relationships, his dad, mom, stepmother, stepfather, grandmother, band members and a host of other relatives, friends and fans. The headline in the Hampton, VA newspaper read "Hampton Singer Walt Redmond, Jr, 35 Dies of Drug Overdose". It was such a sad time.

The funeral was a beautiful tribute to Walt. It was the largest funeral that we had ever seen at that church. In fact, we had a video feed set up in the adjacent Family Life Center so that the people who were not able to get inside the church could still be a part of the service. There were over 400 people in attendance.

Jeff does a great funeral. He projects pictures of the deceased onto a large video screen. He did this with pictures of Walt beginning with baby pictures and spanning his entire lifetime. He played a video of Walt performing the song "PRAYERS" that he had shared during a worship service just three weeks prior. It was almost like he was there. The last picture we saw of Walt, at the close of the service, was a black and white photograph of him walking down a railroad track, back to the camera, carrying his guitar. It was a beautiful picture. I will always remember it. I have it in my mind as Walt leaving this world and going to heaven to be with the Lord. I know he is there. I know that the drugs cannot hurt him now. I know that he does not need or want them anymore. I know he is at peace in his new eternal life with Jesus.

30

OUTLANDISH COMPLAINTS

The Church, like this great country, is a melting pot of different types of people, different races, social statuses, political views and personalities. There are needy people, self-sufficient people, giving people and loving people. There are people that appear to be who they actually are not and people who do not appear to be who they truly are. The church **IS** full of hypocrites and sinners. The difference between the church and the rest of the world is that the church is full of hypocrites and sinners that KNOW they are hypocrites and sinners. Still, they are trying to live for Christ. They are trying to make a difference in the world. They are trying to be forgiving people and praying for forgiveness themselves. They are trying to share God's love for all people. They do not claim to be "good" people, "perfect" people, "better than someone else" people or any other stereotypical name tags that seem to get hung around their necks. A Christian's only claim is this:

"God loves them and has died so that they can be forgiven for their sins." Therefore, they will love you regardless of whom or what you are.

With that said, there are always people in the Church, as are anywhere, that are mean, vindictive, petty, judgmental and basically, just unhappy. Every church has them, and every minister must deal with them. And that is not all. Some of the complainers that must be dealt with *are not even* members of the church. They just happen to live in the neighborhood. Perhaps they have been bothered by something the minister or church has done.

Of course, some complaints are legitimate and should certainly be dealt with, but some are just outright ridiculous!

One such instance involved a woman that lived in the same neighborhood in which our parsonage was located. The other neighbors had dubbed the woman "the lawn Nazi". This woman seemed to have an unnatural passion for lawn work. So much so that she would walk around the neighborhood with her broom and weed eater, trimming sidewalks and sweeping up piles of clippings for resident(s) to pick up. At first, she appeared to be acting out of kindness but as time went on, she began to get pushy and annoying. Her yen for yard work was beginning to look more and more like an obsession. If you did not pick up the piles, left on your sidewalk, she would leave notes on your door.

As fate would have it, Jeff is not a "yard" person. However, the lawn was mowed weekly. Occasionally, maybe twice in summer months, the edger came out, the sidewalks were neatly trimmed, and the hedges were clipped. Regrettably, for all involved, this was completely unacceptable to the self-appointed neighborhood lawn inspector.

One summer, she repeatedly and anonymously called the church to complain about the condition of the yard. Someone from the church parsonage committee would come over to look at the lawn, deem it acceptable and go on their merry way. This, however, was not going to do for the lawn obsessed neighbor. She would continue to call the church until she got a sympathetic ear. Of course, this bothered Jeff, as he was doing his best to juggle family issues and church issues as well as maintain the lawn. He suspected who was making the calls but did not have proof. Then one day she happened to call someone who had "caller ID". Her cover was blown! Jeff immediately called her and asked her not to call the church anymore. He informed her that even though the church owned the property, he was responsible for the lawn. If she had a problem, he would appreciate it if she would call him! He explained to her that he had a lot of things going on, including caring for his spouse who had cancer and that extensive lawn work was not his priority! She did not care. She informed him that she had seen teenage boys at the house and one of them could do the lawn work. Jeff was angry but retained his cool. Once more, he asked her not to bother the church again and then hung up the telephone.

The next day, there was a knock at the door. Jeff opened it and there stood the Lawn Nazi. She thrust a letter at him and then abruptly turned and walked away. The handwritten letter informed the Jeff that he was "inviting crime into the neighborhood" because he did not keep his lawn edged. (Keep in mind that the yard *was* mowed weekly.) In the letter, she that she would not call the church anymore and she would not bother him again. "Yes!" He thought, "Mission accomplished! Free at last! No more harassment from the Lawn Nazi. It was a reason to celebrate, but alas it was not to be. His celebratory mood was premature.

The calls to the church did stop. She did stop sweeping up piles and leaving them to be picked up by the minister. However, she now began calling the "City Compliance" department to complain about anything and everything.

In one telephone call she complained about a small amount (three handfuls) of pine straw that had blown or been kicked onto the sidewalk. We had very large pine trees in the front yard. She told the city that the sidewalk was obstructed, causing her a problem when she walked in the neighborhood. The city is required to follow up on every complaint, so following the telephone call, came another knock on the door. There stood a gentleman who identified himself as a compliance officer for the city.

"I know this is ridiculous and I hate to even say anything, but I am required to follow up on all complaints. Apparently, someone thinks that the pine straw on the sidewalk in front of your house is causing a problem," He said.

"May I ask who called in the complaint?" asked Jeff.

"We're not allowed to divulge that information sir," he replied.

"That's okay; I think I know who it was."

They walked out to the sidewalk together and kicked the pine straw back up into the grass.

"Thank you, sir, I'm sorry to have bothered you," and with that, he left.

Jeff realized that the harassment was not going to stop. Someone called the city about his family's vehicles, that were seemingly, parked more than twelve inches from the curb. Apparently, there is a law about how far away from the curb you can park a vehicle. She was probably out there with a tape measure!

Another time, one of Jeff's sons went outside to go to work and found a tow sticker on his windshield, indicating that his car had not been moved in weeks and was abandoned. The sticker indicated that if the vehicle were not moved in the next two days, it would be towed away. The car was driven daily to and from work! Yes, it was parked in the same place every day, as were all the family cars. Apparently, someone, whom we suspected was "The Lawn Nazi", thought it never moved...or did she?

In yet another instance, the police were called the day after an inspection sticker expired on one of the family cars. We had not noticed, but someone sure did! The complaints never stopped for us. I hope and pray that she was kinder to the next parsonage family.

31

Oh God, Please No More
Meetings

Most ministers will agree that their least favorite part of their job is the meetings. Churches like to meet. They have many committees. Each hs its own set of responsibilities and committee members. Each one thinks that it is the most important when it comes to decision making. They sometimes forget that they are supposed to be acting on behalf of the church members and not their own opinions, wants and needs.

Ministers are not fond of meetings for several reasons.

1. They seem to go on forever.
2. They don't usually accomplish much.
3. Ninety-five percent take place in the evenings.
4. Surprisingly, people are not always nice!

Number four leads me to the next story. Jeff was at a Staff Parish Relations committee meeting one evening and it was not going well. This church had been established fifty years prior and had grown out of a high crime area with neighborhood gangs. It had a reputation for being difficult. The church tried to do good but there was much in-fighting. Some years before Jeff was appointed here, the DS had stopped holding yearly Charge Conference meetings at the church due to continual fist fights.

On this evening the committee met to go over the pastors yearly review. Some members were not happy that Jeff was making changes in the church. He had started using more up-beat music and different types of media during Sunday morning services. Attendance had grown and they were reaching out to the community. They led people to Christ. They Baptized new members. What was not to like? Change! Some people do not like change.

One of the committee members shouted at Jeff and compared him to Hitler and Mussolini declaring that wars had been fought to get rid of people like Jeff! He was angry because Jeff was enforcing the "Order of the Discipline" regarding appointing new officers. After the committee member used the "F" word, Jeff promptly dismissed the meeting. The following week, the same man invited Jeff to his granddaughter's birthday party. He had already moved on.

Not all meetings are this outrageous. Most are dull, uneventful and unproductive.

KAREN CANNON

32

A Letter to the Bishop (It is all about me!)

One church member mailed a letter to the Bishop, complaining on behalf of themselves and three or four other members, of a 300 active member congregation, that the minister had made changes to the worship service and the music program.

The person complained that the minister was phasing out the choir and was "destroying our Methodist traditions". This person was also holding the minister responsible for the departure of three music directors during his seven-year appointment. The person thought that she, who was a choir member, should be consulted about personnel issues regarding the Choir Director. She felt that the choir directors either left or were asked to leave because the minister did not like them. Since she was not on the personnel committee, she was unaware that the first director left because she was not happy with the inclusion of "praise" music. She was not interested in playing or directing anything other than traditional music and therefore applied and was hired at a more traditional church. The other two choir directors left because of personal and performance issues.

The complainer was also upset about the addition of "Children's Church" in the Sunday Service. I guess she did not think it was important for children to be exposed to the church environment. The complainer felt that this five-minute message, during the Sunday Service, was keeping children and their parents from going to Sunday school. Of course, this is obviously a ridiculous conclusion.

But wait, there is more!!! She then asked for clarification regarding the minister's tenure and vacation time that could be taken at his discretion. I am not sure why she felt this was needed information unless she wanted to determine when the minister could take vacation or personal time.

The complainer ended the letter by offering the opinion that the minister "should be moved to a congregation that better fits him".

This was less than a dozen people speaking for the masses. This minister had doubled the size of the congregation since his arrival, seven years earlier. He had baptized a record number of babies and brought in a slew of new members, many on profession of faith and as first-time church members.

The Bishop received the letter, looked at it and called the minister. The Bishop's response was "If a member has an issue, it needs to be taken up with the Pastor Parish Relations committee at the church, not the Bishop." The Bishop indicated that this kind of letter is received now and again, usually from a member that is not able to control things to their liking, and that they would not respond at this level. The matter, if there was one, would have to be handled by the Pastor Parish Relations committee.

The matter was then dropped, and the letter was discussed at the church level. Nothing became of the complaint. But as is with most complainers, the letter writer was still unhappy and unable to control the situation. She continued to be a "thorn in the flesh" continuously trying to stir up discontent among the church people. She was largely unsuccessful but nonetheless, an annoyance. Just so happens that the minister had already served seven years at this church and as was his usual pattern, was ready to move to his next appointment. When the time came, he requested a new appointment, and one was granted. The minister figured that the complainer probably thought he left because of the complaints that had been filed. That was far from the truth, but if it made, her feel better, than so be it!

33

The Next Chapter

Jeff's time as a full-time pastor is coming to an end. He is ready for retirement. For real this time. I think! He actually did retire two years ago.

It is frowned upon for a retired minister to attend a church he once served, so we were visiting area churches trying to find one we liked. One Sunday we decided to drive to Poquoson VA and try a Methodist church there. Our very first Sunday the serving pastor said to Jeff, "I think I know you." Jeff said, "I have just retired from the ministry." The pastor asked Jeff if he would be interested in filling in for him for a Sunday, as he was getting ready to go on four weeks of leave. He had a few people lined up but could use the help. Jeff said sure. What we did not know was that the serving pastor had cancer. Jeff filled in for two weeks and the church members really liked him. A month later, the pastor could no longer conduct the Sunday service, due to his health and he asked Jeff to fill in. Sadly, the pastor passed away and the DS allowed Jeff to stay. We have been serving this church for almost two and a half years. Jeff says he is ready to retire now, but I am not so sure. We will have to wait and see where God leads him. I think mentally he is ready to move on to the next chapter in his life. Like most retirees, he wants to travel, relax and do nothing, The bottom line is this. It's not time until God says it time.

34

Questions for Jeff

1. **What is your favorite thing about your job?** There is a lot of variety. Each day holds something different. Never boring.
2. **What is your least favorite thing about your job?** Experiencing people's pain and sadness.
3. **What other jobs have you had?** Summer intern at the shipyard during college, assistant city manager, probation officer, youth director, associate dean of students and chaplain, police chaplain, hospital chaplain. Most of my other jobs coincide with being in some type of ministry, i.e. local pastor, associate pastor or elder pastor.
4. **What question are you asked most often?** Can I be forgiven for the things I have done?
5. **What is the most difficult recurring task that you often deal with?** Counseling parents having trouble with their children. Mostly teenagers.
6. **What is your favorite recurring task or situation that you often deal with?** Destination weddings and bap-

tisms. I do not do a lot of destination weddings, but when I do, they are fun! One of our friends had fallen in love with a highly decorated French Officer who had been stationed in Norfolk for four years. They got married in Key West Florida. It was a beautiful destination and I got to perform a ceremony for two of our favorite people. The weather was beautiful, the beach was beautiful, the bride was breathtaking. The groom looked good too. There was one moment, following the wedding, that stood out from the rest. We were taking pictures after the ceremony. The Sun was shining on the white sandy beach, waves gently splashing on the rocks, camera shutters clicking when right through the middle, between the cameras and the bride and groom, struts a man wearing a men's suspender thong. If you do not know what that is, you must Google it. Trust me, it is worth it. Both embarrassing and comical.

Baptisms are also a favorite. I love bringing new babies into the fold. So much hope and promise. I also like to remind people that we do not, in the Methodist denomination, christen babies. We christen ships. We BAPTIZE babies!

7. **What is the most interesting situation that you have had to deal with?** I was once called to a home to intervene with a lady that had her mother tied to a chair and was going to kill her. Also, counseling sessions can turn

into interesting situations.

8. **What was your most unusual funeral?** I did a funeral for a young man that died from an accidental gunshot wound. He had been an avid motorcycle rider and had many, many friends. Prior to the funeral we began to hear rumblings about there being some kind of disturbance during the service. The rumor was that some people were going to come armed with weapons. .As a result, we had to have police officers attend the service. It was a very stressful time for me, the family and the officers. Thankfully, there were not any incidences. In tribute to the young man, his motorcycle was parked in the Narthex during the funeral and afterwards a long procession of motorcycle riders followed the body to the cemetery. It was both very loud and a touching tribute.

9. **What has been your favorite church?** Always the one I am currently serving!

10. **Would you do this all over again?** Yes!

11. **What would you do differently?** In my early years, I tended to be more judgmental. I would purposefully try to be more grace filled. I have learned that there truly are two sides to every story, and that you cannot truly understand someone's situation unless you have walked in their shoes. One such situation presented itself to me

when my wife was diagnosed with cancer. I had counseled and spent many hours with people who had cancer. I spent time with their families. I cried with them. I prayed with them. I encouraged them. I thought I had walked in their shoes. I had been with so many. Then my wife was diagnosed. It was a sucker punch to the gut. I was scared. I was angry. We had only been married nine months. How could this be happening? I realized that I really had NOT had any idea how it felt. Now I do. Now I am better equipped to help other.